Social Differentiation in Cameroon English

BERKELEY
INSIGHTS
IN LINGUISTICS
AND SEMIOTICS

Irmengard Rauch
General Editor

Vol. 70

PETER LANG
New York • Washington, D.C./Baltimore • Bern
Frankfurt am Main • Berlin • Brussels • Vienna • Oxford

ALOYSIUS NGEFAC

Social Differentiation in Cameroon English

Evidence from Sociolinguistic Fieldwork

PETER LANG
New York • Washington, D.C./Baltimore • Bern
Frankfurt am Main • Berlin • Brussels • Vienna • Oxford

Library of Congress Cataloging-in-Publication Data

Ngefac, Aloysius.
Social differentiation in Cameroon English:
Evidence from sociolinguistic fieldwork / Aloysius Ngefac.
p. cm. — (Berkeley insights in linguistics and semiotics; v. 70)
Includes bibliographical references.
1. English language—Cameroon. 2. English language—Social aspects—Cameroon.
3. Language and culture—Cameroon. 4. Cameroon—Languages. I. Title.
PE3442.C3N53   427.96711—dc22   2008024752
ISBN 978-1-4331-0390-2
ISSN 0893-6935

Bibliographic information published by **Die Deutsche Bibliothek**.
Die Deutsche Bibliothek lists this publication in the "Deutsche
Nationalbibliografie"; detailed bibliographic data is available
on the Internet at http://dnb.ddb.de/.

© 2008 Peter Lang Publishing, Inc., New York
29 Broadway, 18th floor, New York, NY 10006
www.peterlang.com

To the Almighty God in whose hands my destiny lies;

To my beloved father, Mbe Robert Ajua, who travelled to the world of the ancestors;

TO my dear mother, Mama Joana Amomoh, who has always taken good care of me;

To my dear wife, Patricia Ngefac, who has a profound love for me;

To my dear daughter, Ajua Daniela Ngefac, and my beloved sons, Temate Edgar Ngefac and Amomoh Jonathan-Irving, who are our bumbles of joy.

Table of Contents

Preface

This book introduces a new dimension of studying English in Cameroon, a new ecological setting that is significantly different from most Western contexts. Instead of studying Cameroon English by describing the deviations from mother tongue varieties of English, such as British English, as has been the case in most previous studies on this variety of English, this book focuses, principally, on the patterns of correlation between some social categories and features of Standard British English, the variety of English presumed to be the target in the ELT industry in Cameroon. The study of Cameroon English from the perspective of comparing sociolinguistic patterns in Cameroon to those reported in mother tongue English contexts is a further attempt to demonstrate that the English language in a New English context, such as Cameroon, has taken a significantly different shape from what obtains in an Inner Circle English environment, such as the UK.

The promotion of Standard British English or any mother tongue English in the Cameroonian classroom at this point in time, to the detriment of Cameroon English, is an indication that policy makers and curriculum designers have not taken into consideration the twists and turns the language has undergone in Cameroon. The English language in Cameroon is actually rooted in her historical, ecological, cultural and sociolinguistic realities. The obvious consequence of attempting to implant a Western model of English in Cameroon or attempting to assess Cameroonian speakers in terms of their knowledge of a Western model of English will always yield results that are significantly different from those reported in the West, as the results of this investigation clearly show. Instead of castigating Cameroon English as a concoction of mistakes and targeting features of a variety of English (such as Standard British English) that is psychologically, physically and practically far remote from many Cameroonians, Cameroon English can be standardized and promoted in the classroom. If this variety of English was already standardized and the informants of this study were evaluated in terms of their knowledge of its standard features, there is no doubt that most of the sociolinguistic patterns reported in the Western world would be observable in the Cameroonian context.

This book also studies the impact of a speaker's mood on the quality of his or her speech. In a very sophisticated and creative methodological approach, the speech of some informants was studied in their moods of anger, fear and joy. It is therefore claimed in this book that, in addition to traditional sociolinguistic categories (gender, age, ethnicity, etc.), the mood of a speaker can determine describable linguistic variability, especially if speakers are evaluated in terms of their knowledge of a language or a variety of a language that is in harmony with their souls.

The process to come up with this book involved many stages and many challenges, which could not be overcome without assistance from many people. My heart-felt gratitude goes to Professor Edgar W. Schneider of the University of Regensburg and Professor Augustin Simo Bobda of the University of Yaounde I who supervised the research project that I later on converted to this book. For Professor Edgar Schneider, I cannot adequately express my gratitude to him for the support he has continued to give me since I left his Department in 2001 and for the fatherly way in which he actually accommodated me at his Department.

My special gratitude also goes to Professor Paul Mbangwana, Dr. Alexander Kautzsch, Professor Magnus Huber, Mrs Patricia Ngefac and Dr. Schleburg Florian. They have made tremendous sacrifices at different points in time to help me and I continue to rely on their assistance for most of my accomplishments, including this book.

My profound gratitude also goes to the German Academic Exchange Service (DAAD) for granting me an award to complete my doctorate dissertation in Germany. I am also particularly indebted to the Fulbright organization for awarding me a postdoctoral scholarship to conduct research and give occasional lectures at different US institutions of higher learning.

I am highly indebted to Professor Gillian Sankoff who made my US experience very enriching, exciting and memorable. She played the role of a mother, a very good friend and a facilitator. I also enjoyed the company of Professor William Labov and that of the entire Faculty of the Department of Linguistics at the University of Pennsylvania.

My special thanks also go to my informants whose speech provided the raw data needed for the study. I am particularly grateful to the informants whose speech was recorded without their knowledge.

Aloysius Ngefac

August 2008

Abbreviations

CamE: Cameroon English
CEPE:Certificat d'Etudes Premaire et Elementaire
CS: Casual Style
ELT: English Language Teaching
FS: Formal Style
FSLC: First School Leaving Certificate
GambE: Gambian English
GhanE: Ghambian English
GCE: General Certificate of Education
HSs: High Status Speakers
J: Journalists
KenE: Kenyan English
LSs: Low Status Speakers
LWC: Lower Working Class
LMC: Lower Middle Class
MD: Medical Doctors
MC: Middle Class
MMC: Middle Middle Class
MP: Minimal Pairs
MWC: Middle Working Class
NEs: New Englishes
n.d.: No date
NigHE: Nigerian Hausa English
NigIE: Nigerian Igbo English
NigYE: Nigerian Yoruba English
P: Postgraduate students
PRS: Passage Reading Style
RP: Received Pronunciation
S: Secondary School Students
SAE: Southern African (Black) English
SBE: Standard British English
SLE: Sierra Leonean English
SRS: Sentence Reading Style
SudE: Sudanese English
TanzE: Tanzanian English
U: Undergraduate students
UMC: Upper Middle Class

UWC: Upper Working Class
WC: Working Class
WLS: Word List Style

Phonetic Symbols Used

CamE Vowels

Monophthongs	Example	Transcription
/i/	sit, seat	/sit/
/e/	Mary	/meri/
/ɛ/	penal	/pɛnal/
/a/	cat, cart	/kat/
/ɔ/	pot, port	/pɔt/
/o/	post	/post/
/u/	pull, pool	/pul/

Diphthongs	Example	Transcription
/ie, iə/	chair	/tʃie/, /tʃiə/
/iɔ/	period	/piriɔt/
/ue/	fuel	/fuel/

consonants	Example	Transcription
/p/	pull	/pul/
/b/	bag	/bak/
/t/	tour, bad	/tɔ/, /bat/
/d/	dog	/dɔk/
/k/	cat, dog	/kat/, /dɔk/
/s/	Joseph	/ʤosef/
/z/	increasing	/inkrizin/
/n/	singing	/singin/
/l/	liquid	/likwit/

SBE vowels used

Monophthongs	Example	Transcription
/ɪ/	sit	/sɪt/
/iː/	seat	/siːt/
/ɛ/	sector	/sɛktə/
/æ/	happy	/hæpɪ/
/ɑː/	cart	/kɑːt/
/ɒ/	pot	/pɒt/

/ɔː/	port	/pɔːt/
/ʌ/	drugs	/drʌgz/
/ʊ/	pull	/pʊl/
/uː/	pool	/puːl/
/ɜː/	hard working	/hɑːdwɜːkɪŋ/
/ɔ/	cupboard	/kʌbəd/

Diphthongs	Example	Transcription
/eɪ/	satan	/seɪtn/
/ɛə/	Mary	/mɛərɪ/
/ɪə/	mere	/mɪə/
/ʊə/	fuel	/fjʊəl/
/əʊ/	post	/pəʊst/
/aɪ/	buy	/baɪ/
/aʊ/	cow	/kaʊ/

consonants	Example	Transcription
/p/	port	/pɔːt/
/b/	beet	/biːt/
/t/	typist	/taɪpɪst/
/k/	cat	/kæt/
/g/	single	/sɪŋg (ə)l/
/ʤ/	journey	/ʤɜːnɪ/
/tʃ/	teacher	/tiːtʃə/
/f/	forum	/fɒrəm/
/v/	of	/ɒv/
/θ/	third	/θɜːd/
/ð/	that	/ðæt/
/s/	nursery	/nɜːsərɪ/
/z/	president	/prɛzɪdənt/
/ʃ/	short	/ʃɔːt/
/ʒ/	usual	/juːʒʊəl/
/h/	how	/haʊ/
/m/	murmur	/məːmə/
n/	no	/nəʊ/
/ŋ/	singing	/sɪŋɪŋ/
/l/	learn	/lɜːn/
/r/	read	/riːd/
/j/	population	/pɒpjʊleɪʃn/
/w/	work	/wɜːk/

General Introduction

This book is an investigation on the correlation between English phonological variables and some social categories in Cameroon, a New English context, which has sociopolitical, economic, cultural, sociolinguistic and linguistic realities that are different from those of Western industrialized contexts. Some of the social categories considered in the scope of this study have actually been given in-depth investigations in the Western world where English is generally used as a mother-tongue. But it is hypothesized and claimed in this study that Western English societies and New English contexts, such as Cameroon, do not have the same linguistic and socio-cultural realities and, as a result, the correlation patterns between linguistic variables and some of the sociolinguistic categories in a New English community, such as Cameroon, may not reflect the patterns reported in the Western world. It is for this reason that Kachru (1992: 11) recommends that "it is indeed essential to recognise that World Englishes represent certain linguistic, cultural and pragmatic realities and pluralism, and that pluralism is now an integral part of World Englishes and literatures written in Englishes".

Interestingly, in spite of the many twists and turns the English language has undergone in Cameroon, because of her sociolinguistic and cultural realities, traditional native English norms, especially those of Standard British English (SBE), continue to be the target in the English Language Teaching (ELT) industry in Cameroon. The ELT contents and the nature of official examinations prove that typical Cameroon English features are relegated to the background and those of British English are highly prioritized. It is not surprising that in the preface of one of the most widely recommended textbooks in Cameroon, entitled *Watch Your English!*, the author states that

> While acknowledging the legitimate emergence of an autonomous variety of English in Cameroon, I believe that we are still, in many ways, dependent upon British and American norms. Our educational and professional successes are still dependent on these norms. (Bobda 2002:v)

In spite of the belief that SBE or any other Western variety of English is actually promoted on the Cameroonian landscape, numerous studies (see, for example, Masanga 1983, Mbangwana 1987, Kouega 1991, Bobda 1994, Atechi 1996 and Ngefac 2005) have demonstrated that Cameroon English is systematically and predictably different from Western Englishes (e.g. British and American English), especially at the phonological level. If educational authorities continue to insist on SBE norms, it implies that they are explicitly or implicitly making a choice on what should constitute prestige English linguistic features in Cameroon, which, according to such a school of thought, should be those of the variety of English officially recommended in Cameroon.

The wish to continue targeting British or American English norms in Cameroon, as expressed in the above quotation, may or may not be quite legitimate, but one of the fundamental issues we wish to investigate in this study is whether prestige linguistic features of the variety of English recommended in Cameroon are likely to correlate with some sociolinguistic categories in a way similar to what has been reported in studies conducted in the Western world (e.g. Fischer 1958; Labov 1966, 1972; Wolfram 1969; Trudgill 1972, 1974 and Macaulay 1976, 1977, Coates 1986, Chambers 1995).

This study is a sociophonological investigation and the phonological scope is limited to segments and stress. As revealed in previous literature, the systematic and predictable peculiarities of most New Englishes are most glaring in the areas of segments and stress. The sociolinguistic scope includes the following extra-linguistic categories: level of education, gender, occupation, age, ethnicity, regionality, phonological style and the mood of a speaker.

The sociolinguistic significance of the study is multidimensional. First, the correlation patterns reported in the Western world are further evaluated in a New English context. Second, the study of Cameroon English within the context of some sociolinguistic categories is a further attempt to show that ELT goals in Cameroon should be redefined by considering that the development and use of the language in such a context is sanctioned by the ecological, historical, cultural and sociolinguistic realities of the place. If British or American English norms continue to be the target in Cameroon, it implies that the twists and turns the language has undergone in Cameroon, because of numerous contextual factors, are completely ignored by curriculum designers. Third, the study provides further evidence for the existence of a variety of English that is significantly different from Western varieties of English. Fourth, the study of speech in terms of the mood of a speaker is, in fact, a sociolinguistic innovation which has not been attempted in many sociolinguistic studies.

Besides the General Introduction, the work is divided into five chapters. The General Introduction presents the purpose, the scope and the sociolinguistic significance of the study. It equally presents the highlights of the different chapters.

Chapter One appreciates and analyses the literature on the New Englishes. It is argued and exemplified, through such aspects as features, intelligibility, attitude and pedagogical concerns, that the existence of the New Englishes is no more a doubtful reality. The chapter also presents literature on Cameroon English, the variety of English upon which the investigation is based.

Chapter Two is a critical review of previous sociolinguistic patterns. A survey of sociolinguistic literature is made and the theories and principles, upon which the studies are based, are critically evaluated. Another preoccupation of the chapter is an evaluation of the extent to which the investigation differs from previous ones. In this attempt, the contribution of the study is unequivocally underscored.

The third chapter is devoted to method-related issues. The issues include a description of the informants, a presentation of the instruments for data collection, the method for data collection, a presentation and description of the data and the method of data analysis.

The fourth chapter presents the findings of the investigation according to the various social categories under study. In each case, an attempt is made to account for the correlation pattern that emerges.

The fifth chapter focuses on the conclusion of the work. The highlights of the findings are succinctly recapitulated and a further attempt is made to situate the findings within existing sociolinguistic knowledge.

Chapter One
The New Englishes

1. Introduction

The English language was transported and transplanted in new ecological settings through colonialism and other routes. In these new settings, the language has undergone many twists and turns dictated by the historical, ecological, sociolinguistic and cultural realities of such places. The inevitable and natural consequence of this situation is the fact that the language has acquired diverse phonological, syntactic and lexico-semantic patterns and realities that reflect different areas of the globe and these peculiarities are significantly different from those of older Englishes (British and American English, for instance). The recognition that the language is no more the preserve of a few countries, such as Britain and the United States, has, in recent years, resulted in expressions such as "Global English", "World Englishes", "International English", "English World-Wide" and "New Englishes". The language has therefore emerged as a universal language with distinctive pragmatic, cultural and linguistic realities reflecting different parts of the world (see Kachru 1986).

The global status of the language has been acknowledged by different authors. Kachru (1985, 1986) has discussed the situation of English in the world in terms of three concentric circles: the "Inner Circle", the "Outer Circle" and the "Expanding Circle". The 'Inner Circle' refers to countries where English is used predominantly as a mother tongue. These countries include the United Sates, Britain, Canada, Australia and New Zealand. The 'Outer Circle' comprises former British and American colonies where English has developed a wide range of functions. In such contexts, English has become the language of administration, education, governance, literary creativity and popular culture. The 'Outer Circle' countries include, but not limited to, Bangladesh, Ghana, India, Kenya, Malaysia, Nigeria, Pakistan, Philippines, Singapore and Zambia. The 'Expanding Circle' refers to those countries where English is used for specific functions and the functions are more limited than what is obtained in the 'Outer Circle'. Such countries include China, Egypt, Indonesia, Israel, Japan, Korea, Saudi Arabia, Taiwan, USSR, Zimbabwe and Nepal. Kachru's three concentric circles, in fact, compete with the traditional classification as ENL (English as a Native language), ESL (English as a Second language) and EFL (English as a Foreign language) respectively, but Kachru and Nelson (1996:79) argue that such terminologies as ENL, ESL and EFL create attitudinal problems as one is likely to think that ESL and EFL speakers occupy an inferior position to the one occupied by "native" or ENL speakers.

Crystal (1998:357) has identified 48 different countries, drawn from all the seven continents of the planet earth, in which English has an official status. This is an indication that the English language has transcended many regional and international frontiers. McArthur (1998:97) has also exemplified the global status of English in terms of a circle. He describes the circle as

> A wheel with a hub, spokes, and rim. The hub is called World Standard English, within an encircling band of regional varieties, such as the standard and other forms of African English, American English, Canadian English and Irish English. Beyond these, but linked to them by spokes marking off eight regions of the world, is a crowded (even riotous) fringe of sub-varieties   such as Aboriginal English, Black English Vernacular, Gullah, Jamaican Nation Language, Krio, Singapore English, and Ulster Scots. (McArthur 1998:97)

Within the picture of English in the world, Outer Circle varieties have been referred to in the literature as *New Englishes*. Kachru (1985) sees the English spoken in the Expanding Circle as performance varieties, which cannot be classified as *New Englishes* because they have not yet developed systematic indigenized linguistic peculiarities like what is observed in the Outer Circle. The main preoccupation of this chapter is, therefore, to underscore the notion of New Englishes which is particularly relevant in this study because the investigation is based, to a very large extent, on the hypothesis that indigenized varieties of English and traditional mother tongue Englishes have distinctive social and linguistic realities and, as a result, tend to have different correlation patterns between linguistic and social variables. Such issues as features, intelligibility, attitudes (status) and pedagogical concerns would be the principal concerns of this chapter. Another preoccupation of the chapter includes a particular focus on CamE, the variety of English under investigation. We shall start the discussion with the question of whether the New Englishes actually display distinctive linguistic peculiarities to be considered different from Western varieties of English.

1.1 Linguistic Peculiarities of the New Englishes

Writers from different parts of the world have reported that the existence of the New Englishes is now an unquestionable reality – a situation that was highly debatable in the times of Prator (1968) who saw features of non-native Englishes as cancerous tumours or havoc that was threatening the health of traditional native Englishes. The New Englishes, in fact, manifest their distinctiveness from older Englishes through a number of systematic and predictable processes at all linguistic levels, but we shall limit our discussion to the domain of phonology since the scope of the study does not include other levels of language.

Some of the phonological processes through which the New Englishes (henceforth NEs) systematically and predictably display their uniqueness from older Englishes include the replacement of segments, the simplification of consonant clusters through vowel epenthesis, the deletion of final consonants and deviant placement of stress. These processes have been amply exemplified in the numerous studies on the NEs (see, for instance, Bamgbose 1971, Sey 1973, Platt et al. 1984, Kachru 1985, 1986, Schmied 1991, and Bobda 1994). With reference to some of these studies, it would be underscored how these new varieties of English manifest their distinctiveness from traditional native Englishes through the above-mentioned phonological processes.

1.1.1 Replacement of Segments. The replacement of traditional native English segments is one of the ways through which the NEs manifest their distinctiveness from older varieties of English (e.g. British English and American English). This replacement is observed in accents across regional and international boundaries. It should be noted right from the outset that, in reporting the way the 'deviant' segments are distributed, some scholars have run the risk of over-generalisation and this justifies why opinions tend to differ on how some of the features are distributed across boundaries.

The NURSE vowel which corresponds to RP /ɜː/ and General American English /ɜr/ is one of the most widely investigated segments used to show how the NEs deviate from mother tongue Englishes. Bobda (2000: 41), after Wells (1982), considers the NURSE vowel as the vowel shared by NURSE words such as "hurt", "term" "work", and "learn". In all studies which include RP /ɜː/ in the scope of their investigations (e. g. Hancock and Angogo 1982, 1984; Görlach and Holm 1986 and Schmied 1991), there is a unanimous view that speakers of these indigenized Englishes replace it in all phonological environments and in all lexical items to yield sounds completely different from mother tongue English variants. This tendency has been observed in all African accents of English, Caribbean English, Indian English, Singaporean English and other localized varieties. There is no challenge to this view. But the question of how /ɜː/ is replaced in the different New Englishes remains highly controversial.

Hancock and Angogo (1982) and Schmied (1991), for instance, maintain that RP /ɜː/ in the word "bird" is replaced with /ɔ/ in West African Englishes and /a/ in the Englishes of East Africa, yielding /bɔd/ and /bad/ respectively. But Bobda (2000d: 44f) persuasively argues that such a view is an over-generalisation. For the case of West African Englishes, he establishes that the realization of RP /bɜːd/ as /bɔd/ cannot be considered as the general pronunciation in West African Englishes. He unambiguously demonstrates that RP /bɜːd/ is pronounced as /bɔd/ only in Gambian English, Sierra Leonean English and Nigerian Yoruba English. He also reveals that in Ghanaian English, Nigerian Igbo English and Cameroon English, /bɜːd/ is realised as /bɛd/. In Nigerian Hausa English, it is realised as /bad/. One can notice that only within Nigeria, as many as three different pronunciations for the NURSE vowel in "bird" can be identified.

As concerns the case of East African Englishes, Bobda (ibid.) equally contends that RP /ɜː/ in "bird" which is said by previous writers to be realised as /a/ in East African Englishes, yielding /bad/, is also ain instance of over-generalisation. He argues that "Tanzania does not neatly belong to the Eastern group, but rather with Malawi and Zambia, to the transition zone between /a/ and Southern /ɛ/" (Bobda, ibid.). He holds that scholars who have grouped Tanzania with Kenya and Uganda have been tempted "by a host of Tanzania's similarities with Uganda and Kenya (common use of Kiswahili and membership to the East African Community)" (Bobda, ibid). As a conclusion, the author maintains that /bad/ as the pronunciation of RP /bɜːd/ is common with Kenyan and Uganda Englishes and not with Tanzanian English.

Bobda (ibid.) goes further to demonstrate, in greater detail, how the NURSE vowel /ɜː/ is distributed across African accents of English. The following table recapitulates the pronunciation of sample NURSE words across some selected accents of African Englishes.

Table 1a: The pronunciation of / ɜː/ in some African Englishes (quoted from Bobda 2000d: 47)

Word	RP	GamE	SLE	GhanE	NigYE	NigE	NigIE
term	tɜːm	tam	tam	tɛm	tam	tam	tɛm
learn	lɜːn	lan	lan	lɛn	lan	lan	lɛn
transfer	transfɜː	transfa	transfa	tansfɛ	transfa	transfa	tansfa
prefer	prifɜː	prifa	prifa	prifɛ	prifa	prifa	prifɛ
person	pɜːsɔn	pɛsɛn,pɛ-	pɔsɔn,pɛ-	pɛsɔn	pɛsɔn,pɔ-	pasɔn	pɛsɛn
thirty	θɜːtɪ	tati	tati	tɛti	tati	tati	tɛti
thirteen	θɜːtin	tatin	tatin	tɛtin	tatin	tatin	tɛtin
first	fɜːst	fɔst	fɔst	fɛst	fɔst	fast	fɛst
third	θɜːd	tɔd	tɔd	tɛd	tɔd	tad	tɛd
girl	gɜːl	gal, gɛl	g(j)al,gɛl	gɛl	gɛl, gjɛl	gal	gɛl
work	wɜːk	wɔk	wɔk	wɛk	wɔk	wak	wɔk
burn	bɜːn	bɔn	bɔn	bɛn	bɔn	ban	bɔn
murmur	mɜːmɜ	mɔmɔ	mɔmɔ	mɛma	mɔmɔ	mama	mɔmɔ
urban	ɜːbɜn	ɔban	ɔban	ɛbɛn	ɔban	aban	ɔban
journey	dʒɜːnɪ	dʒɔne	dʒɔne	dʒɛne	dʒɔne	dʒane	dʒɔne

Table 1a continues

Word	RP	CamE	SAE	TanzE	KenE	SudE
term	tɜːm	tɛm	tɛm	tɛm	tam	tɛrm
learn	lɜːn	lɛn	lɛn	lɛn	lan	lɛrn
transfer	transfɜː	tansfa	tansfɛ	tansfa,fɛ	transfa	tansfɛr
prefer	prifɜː	prifɛ	prifɛ	prifɛ,fa	prifa	prifɛr
person	pɜːsɜn	pɛsɛn	pɛsɜn	pɛsɜn	pasɜn	pɛrsɛn
thirty	θɜːtɪ	tɛti	tɛti	tɛti	tati	sɛrti
thirteen	θɜːtin	tɛtin	tɛtin	tɛtin	tatin	sɛrtin
first	fɜst	fɛst	fɛst	fast	fast	fɛst
third	θɜːd	tɛd	tɛd	tɛd	tad	sɛrd
bird	bɜːd	bɛd	bɛd	bɛd	bad	bɛrd
girl	gɜːl	gɛl	gɛl	gɛl	gal	gɛrl
firm	fɜːm	fɛm	fɛm	fɛm	fam	fɛrm
work	wɜːk	wɔk	wɛk	wɛk	wak	wɔrk
burn	bɜːn	bɔn,-ɛ	bɛn	ban	ban	bɔrn
murmur	mɜːmɜ	mɔmɔ	mɛma	mama	mama	mɔrmɔr
urban	ɜːbɜn	ɔban	ɛban	aban	aban	ɔrban
journey	dʒɜːnɪ	dʒɔne	dʒɛne	dʒane	dʒane	dʒɔrne

As the table clearly shows, the different West African Englishes which include Gambian English (GamE), Sierra Leonean English (SLE), Ghanaian English (GhanE), Nigerian Yoruba English (NigYE), Nigerian Hausa English (NigHE), Nigerian Igbo English (NigIE) and Cameroon English (CamE) significantly differ in the way they replace the NURSE vowel /ɜː/. It is either replaced with /ɔ/, /a/ or /ɛ/. In Ugandan and Kenyan Englishes, it is replaced with /a/, but in Tanzanian English, it fluctuates between /a/ and /ɛ/ and the tendency for /ɛ/ to be realised is far higher than /a/.The same situation is observed in Zambian and Malawian Englishes, though this is not displayed on the above table. In Southern African (Black) English covering Zimbabwe, Botswana, Namibia, South Africa, Lesotho and Swaziland, /ɜː/ is unambiguously replaced with /ɛ/.

Another tendency observed from the table is the fact that /ɜː/ is not realised at all in any of the Englishes considered. This tendency is also true of Ghanaian English which is often claimed to be closer to traditional native Englishes than the other African Englishes. The absence of RP /ɜː/ in the accents underscored above is a tendency observable in all New Englishes, without an exception (see Platt et al. 1984 and Todd and Hancock 1988). This buttresses the argument that the NEs contrast significantly with native Englishes.

The sound /ʌ/ is another good example of a vowel that is almost systematically replaced in most NEs. Sey (1973: 145) establishes that /ʌ/ is replaced by /ɔ/ in Ghanaian English. But later studies (e. g. Adjaye 1987 and

Bobda 2000a) prove that Ghanaian English speakers systematically replace /ʌ/ with /a/ and not /ɔ/, as previously established. In Nigerian English, Bobda (2000: 258f) joins previous writers like Bamgbose (1971), Jibril (1982) and Awonusi (1986) to report that /ʌ/ is replaced by /ɔ/ in Nigerian Southern English (i. e. the varieties of English spoken in Yoruba and Igbo) and by /a/ in Nigerian Hausa English. He also proves that Sierra Leonean and Cameroonian speakers replace it with /ɔ/. In Kenyan English, /ʌ/ is replaced by /a/, a situation similar to the cases of Ghanaian and Nigerian Hausa Englishes (Bobda 2000a).

The following table, quoted from Bobda (2000a: 263), displays other cases of replacement of RP segments across some selected African Englishes.

Table 1b: Cases of replacement of some RP segments across selected African Englishes (Bobda 2000a:263)

Word	RP	GhanE	SLE	NigSE	NigHE	CamE	KenE
square	skwɛə	skwɛə	skwea, -ia	skwea, -ai	skwea	skwɛ	skwea
beer	bia	bia	bia	Bia	bia	biɛ, biɔ	bia
teacher	tiːtʃə	tiːtʃa	tiːtʃa	tiːtʃa	tiːtʃa	tiːtʃa	tiːtʃa
sector	sɛktə	sɛkta	sɛktɔ	sɛktɔ	sɛkta	sɛktɔ	sɛkta
labour	leɪbə	leba	lebɔ	lebɔ	leba	lebɔ	leba
structure	strʌktʃə	straktʃa	strɔktʃɔ	strɔktʃɔ	straktʃa	strɔktʃɔ	straktʃa
pompous	pɒmpəs	pɔmpas	pɔmpɔs	pɔmpɔs	pɔmpas	pɔmpɔs	pɔmpas
forum	fɔrəm	fɔram	fɔrɔm, um	fɔrɔm, um	fɔram	fɔrɔm	fɔram
formal	fɔːm(ə)l	fɔmal	fɔmal	fɔmal	fɔmal	fɔmal	fɔmɔ(l)
single	sɪŋg(ə)l	siŋgəl	siŋgul	siŋgul	siŋgu(l)	siŋgəl	siŋgɔ(l)
try	traɪ	traɪ	trai	trai	tɔrai	trai	t(ə)rai
quickly	kwɪklɪ	kwikli	kwikli	Kwikli	kwikli	kwikli	kwikili
told us	təuldəs	tolas	tolɔs	tolɔs	tolas	tolɔs	tɔldə as
bring	brɪŋ	briŋ	briŋg	briŋg	briŋg	briŋ	briŋg(i)

As is shown in the table above, almost all RP (accent chosen for reference) segments, especially vowels, are replaced in Ghanaian English (GhanE), Sierra Leonean (SLE), Nigerian Southern English (NigSE), Nigerian Hausa English (NigHE), Cameroon English (CamE) and Kenyan English (KenE). The process of replacement of RP segments is a tendency observable in all NEs. But there is a marked difference in the way these segments are replaced and this is the main point Bobda (ibid.) is emphasizing in the above table. From the table, one can also notice that some previous findings, concerning the way RP segments are replaced, tend to be contradicted. For instance, Platt et al. (1984: 35) establish that the diphthong in RP /biə/ is replaced with /ia/ in West Africa, yielding /bia/. But the tendency is not observable in CamE, as Cameroonian speakers say /biɛ/ or /biə/ (Bobda, 2000:263).

The discussion underscored so far in this section shows that the process of replacement of RP segments is one of the striking ways through which the NEs differ from mother tongue Englishes. It is also underscored that the way the segments are replaced varies from one New English context to another and there is often a tendency for writers to run the risk of over-generalisation by considering a feature to be a peculiarity of a whole region, when, in actual fact, it may vary significantly within a single country (see the case of Nigeria). This does not cancel the fact that some significant similarities are observable in the way these segments are replaced in different New English contexts. For instance, Sierra Leonean English bears a striking resemblance with Nigerian Southern English; Kenyan English is significantly similar to Ugandan English and Ghanaian English also compares Cameroon English in a significant way.

1.1.2 Simplification of Consonant Clusters. In order to manage the heavy syllable structure of English, where there can be as many as three consonants in the onset position and four in the coda position (Bobda 1994), speakers of the NEs tend to rely on the processes of epenthesis and consonant deletion. In West African Englishes, Todd (1986: 288) exemplifies that the words "bottle" and "small", for instance, are pronounced /bɔtul/ or /bɔtɛl/ and /sumul/ respectively. It should be pointed out that the pronunciation of "bottle" as /bɔtul/ and "small" as /sumul/ are not observable in mainstream Cameroon English, and if they do exist at all in CamE, they can only be found at the basilectal end of the continuum. But the pronunciation /bɔtɛl/ very much reflects the general pattern in Cameroon.

In East African English, Hancock and Angogo (1982: 313) also show many instances of simplification of consonants. A good example can be seen in the pronunciation of the word "confidence" which is said to be realised as /kɔnifidɛns/. The insertion of /i/ between /n/ and /f/ is a strategy (process of epenthesis) used by the speakers to ease the articulation of the consonant cluster /nf/ found in the coda position of the first syllable and in the onset position of the second syllable of the word.

A similar situation is revealed in Malaysian English by Wong (1982: 274). In the pronunciation of the word "film", for instance, the vowel /e/ is added to split the consonant cluster. This gives rise to the pronunciation /filem/ for RP /film/. Kachru (1986: 39) also reports another situation which is observed in South Asian Englishes where a vowel is added at word-initial positions to yield pronunciations such as /ɪskul/ and /ɪsteʃan/ for "school" and "station" respectively.

The deletion of consonants is another way through which speakers of NEs simplify consonant clusters. Platt et al. (1984: 43) establish that speakers of

Trinidadian and Indian Englishes tend to delete the second consonant in onset positions to yield pronunciations such as "pobably", "fom", "sill" for "probably", "from" and "still" respectively. They further testify that Hong-Kong and Singaporean speakers of English simplify consonant clusters by deleting the final consonants in words such as "cannot", 'month", "afford", "friend' and "just" to yield "canno", "mon", "affor", "frien" and "jus" respectively.

Todd and Hancock (1986: 96) report a similar tendency in Caribbean English. Words such as "talked", "sand" and "best" are rendered /tɔk/, /san/ and /bes/ respectively. They also point out that the deletion of final consonants is equally a peculiarity of Indian English. One can therefore maintain that most New Englishes simplify consonant clusters at both the onset and coda positions through the processes of epenthesis and deletion of consonants. It would be further examined how the NEs manifest their distinctiveness from native English through deviant stress placement.

1.1.3 Stress Placement in the New Englishes. Generally speaking, the NEs are characterized by two main phenomena. They tend to be syllable-timed and this contrasts with the stressed-timed nature of mother tongue Englishes (see Spencer 1971; Kachru 1984 and Bobda 1994). Crystal (1997: 375) postulates that in a syllable-timed language, the syllables tend to occur at regular intervals of time and this contrasts with a stress-timed language where the "stressed syllables recur at regular intervals of time, regardless of the number of intervening unstressed syllables" (Crystal, ibid.: 365). The rhythm the New Englishes display, having the tendency to be syllable-timed, is logically very different from that displayed by mother tongue Englishes. The second phenomenon which characterizes the stress pattern of the NEs is the fact that they tend to have a forward-stress pattern, though there are number of exceptions to this rule, and contrasts with the general backward stress behaviour of older Englishes. The following examples taken from Bobda and Mbangwana (1993: 209 f) on Cameroon English can be said to reflect the situation in most NEs:

Table 1c: Linguistic items involving a forward stress pattern in CamE

RP	CamE
'annex	an'nex
'barrier	bar'rier
'carton	car'ton
'colleague	col'league
'Agatha	A'gatha
'ancestor	an'cestor
'mattress	mat'tress
'petrol	pe'trol
'Sammy	Sam'my
'salad	Sa'lad
'maintenance	main'tenance
'boycott	boy'cott

(Bobda and Mbangwana 1993:209)

In spite of the forward stress pattern of the above words in CamE, there are a number of lexical items that are stressed initially in CamE, as opposed to the forward stress tendency of the words in mother tongue Englishes. The following examples taken from Bobda and Mbangwana (1993: 211) illustrate:

Table 1d: Linguistic items involving a backward stress pattern in CamE

CamE	RP
'advice	ad'vice
'applause	ap'plause
'estate	est'ate
'professor	pro'fessor
'diskette	dis'kette
'extreme	ex'treme
'synopsis	sy'nopsis
'mosquito	mos'quito

(Bobda and Mbangwana 1993:211)

To sum up the discussion so far on the question of whether the NEs actually have distinctive linguistic peculiarities to be considered different from older Englishes, one can share with previous researchers that these Englishes, in fact, have stable, predictable and systematic linguistic features which make them contrast significantly with traditional Englishes. They actually have the tendency to monophthongize diphthongs, replace central vowels with either front or back vowels, reduce long vowels to short ones and to shift RP stress either forward or backward.

1.2 The Degree of Intelligibility of the New Englishes

The issue of intelligibility of the NEs has been one of the highly debatable issues in international fora and in English language-based scientific publications. In all studies that address the issue (see Bansal 1969, Tiffen 1974, Platt et al. 1984, Honey 1989, Bobda 1994, 2000), there is a unanimous view that the NEs pose serious intelligibility problems to speakers of older Englishes. Brown (1977: 48), quoted in Bobda (2000c: 59), is said to have misunderstood her students who pronounced the word "animism" in *king Lear* as a'nimizəm instead of RP 'ænɪmɪzm. She thought the word the students uttered was *anemia*.

Ikonne (1986: 29) also narrates the frustration a Nigerian woman from a famous Nigerian university went through in the United States as a result of the unintelligibility of her English. Ikonne (ibid.) narrates that

> A Nigerian woman went to do her hair in a saloon owned by an American woman of Jewish extraction. The Nigerian, an English major from a famous Nigerian university, was, of course, sure of her English. She confidently articulated her needs in what she considered Queen's English. Much to her chagrin, however, the only response she drew from the hair dresser was an apology: 'I'm sorry, but I know no foreign language. I speak only English!' Needless to add, the sentences were reinforced with manual gestures as if they were addressed to a deaf and dumb. (Ikonne, ibid.)

It should be remarked that Ikonne's (ibid.) account of the intelligibility problems the Nigerian woman went through is somewhat exaggerated. It is true that the NEs at this point pose serious intelligibility problems to speakers of traditional native Englishes, but the situation has not yet reached the stage where one can claim TOTAL absence of intelligibility as Ikonne (ibid.) is claiming in the above excerpt. If the report is not exaggerated, why should the interlocutor of the Nigerian woman think she was speaking a completely different language, not even a dialect of English? In a realistic situation, a British or an American speaker of English, for instance, may only "strain his /her ears" (Bobda 2000 c: 60) to understand his /her interlocutor speaking a New English, and will not perceive it as a completely different language. One may predict that the situation Ikonne (1986:29) is already precipitating in the above excerpt may only be experienced in some years to come, probably a century or so, where speakers of the NEs and those of older Englishes may not only "strain [their] ears" (Bobda, P.60) to understand each other, but may perceive each other's English as a completely different language. This prediction is buttressed by the fact that the NEs, as revealed by Kachru (1985) and (1986) are constantly undergoing the processes of acculturalisation and indigenisation as steps towards English linguistic autonomy. The prediction cannot, however, be over-emphasized, given that the process of globalisation is almost reducing the whole world into a small village where "we have easy, rapid, and ubiquitous communication, electronic and otherwise [and there is] a strong world-wide will to preserve inter-comprehensibility in English" (Quirk 1985:4).

Cases of intelligibility problems involving mother English speakers and speakers of the NEs are really many. Honey (1989: 104 ff) also reports a situation where there was absence of intelligibility between a British woman and a well-learned Indian scholar when they were on a train in India. It is also revealed that Indian job-seekers in Britain have faced employment problems because of the unintelligibility of their accent. As a condition for Indian medical doctors to be employed in Britain, Honey (ibid.) reveals that their language proficiency was always tested and the results of such tests were not always admirable.

The problem of intelligibility has equally been reported in Cameroon. Talom (1990), for instance, reports that his subjects had no problem understanding features of Cameroon English, but were faced with serious intelligibility problems when the same features were articulated following the RP standard. He read out words such as "attribute", "barrier", "survey", and "plantain" by stressing the words according to RP norms and asked his informants to write down what they heard. Interestingly, words or expressions such as "a tribute", "tribute" were considered by the informants to be RP a'ttribute; "bar", "barrack", "garage" were thought to be RP 'barrier; "sergeant", "service", "said it" were considered as RP 'survey; and "planting" as RP 'plantain. The percentage of the informants who wrote down the right words, articulated with RP stress pattern, was observed to be very minimal.

In an attempt to evaluate the extent to which CamE is intelligible to British and American speakers of English living in Cameroon, Ntumboh (1998: 42) made the following observations, recapitulated in the following table:

Table 1e: The intelligibility of CamE features to British and American speakers of English living in Cameroon

Intelligibility of CamE	British		American		Total	
	No.	%	No.	%	No.	%
1. It is very intelligible	0	0	0	0	0	0
2. It is intelligible	20	41.6	28	58.3	48	26.7
3. It is not very intelligible	65	54.1	55	45.8	120	66.7
4. It is not intelligible	3	25	9	75	12	6.7
5. It is not intelligible at all	0	0	0	0	0	0

(Ntumboh, 1998:42)

The data displayed in the table are very interestingly instructive. It can be noticed that no informant testified that CamE, like any other New English, is very intelligible. A majority of the informants (66.7%) confirmed that CamE, like other NEs, is not very intelligible. As a contrast to Ikonne's (1986) claim, depicted in the excerpt about the experience of the Nigerian woman in the United States, none of the British and American informants declared that CamE was not intelligible at all. One can logically generalise the situation of CamE to the other NEs, though it may not be on a one-to-one basis.

It appears necessary to emphasise that most intelligibility problems between traditional native speakers and speakers of the New Englishes that have been reported in most previous studies are more at the level of pronunciation than at any other linguistic level. This view is confirmed in Ntumboh's (1998) study, where some British and American citizens working in Cameroon were asked to state their opinions on which level of Cameroon English they had problems of intelligibility. The following results were obtained:

Table 1f: Pronunciation as the source of intelligibility problems

Levels	British		American		Total	
	No.	%	No.	%	No.	%
1.) Pronunciation	60	37,5	100	62,5	160	88.9
2.) Grammar/sentence structure	6	50	6	50	12	6,7
3.) Vocabulary	2	25	6	75	8	4,4

(Ntumboh, 1998: 42)

As the table shows, pronunciation accounts for 88.9% of problems of intelligibility to British and American citizens in Cameroon.

To sum up the discussion on intelligibility, one can share with Platt et al. (1984), Kachru (1986) and Bobda (2000c) that the unintelligibility of the NEs is not necessarily a sign of inferiority. One should normally expect the NEs to pose serious intelligibility problems to speakers of other varieties of English if they are said to be undergoing the processes of acculturalisation and indigenisation. In such a situation, if both mother tongue English speakers and those of the NEs do not make conscious efforts to learn each other's English, intelligibility problems will continue to be encountered and a mother English speaker may have to "strain his/ her ears to understand [speakers of the NEs] just as they strain theirs to understand him/her" (Bobda 2000c: 60).

In the face of these intelligibility problems associated with the NEs, which have been reported in different studies, what is likely to be people's attitudes towards such varieties of English? This question introduces the concern of the next section which has to do with attitudes towards these NEs, which have been underscored above to be largely unintelligible, especially to speakers of older Englishes.

1.3 Attitudes towards the New Englishes

The issue of the unintelligibility of the NEs has, in fact, generated many schools of thought. Kachru echoes this situation when he maintains that attitudes and reactions to the different varieties of English "form a spectrum which varies from hilarious attitudinal epithets to a plea for linguistic tolerance" (Kachru, 1986: 100). Interestingly, in this situation, each school of thought claims to be fighting a just cause as none is ready to be influenced by the strong arguments of the other. Bamgbose (1998: 1), quoted in Bobda (2000 c: 54), depicts the peak of this "fight" when "four star generals" in English language scholarship: Lord Randolph Quirk and Professor Braj Kachru (Bamgbose 1998:1) "locked horns at a conference held to mark the 50th anniversary of the British Council" (Bobda 2000c:54). Sir Randolph Quirk is said to have defended the thesis that the need for a global standard and for international intelligibility dictates the maintenance of purity in the English language. Braj Kachru on the other hand argued for the legitimacy and equality of Englishes in the three concentric circles on the basis that English, being a global language, traditional native English speakers cannot continue to be the sole norm setters as if English is their sole property. The two views drummed by Quirk and Kachru introduce two main schools of thought: purism and pragmatism, which would be discussed in greater detail below.

1.3.1 The Attitudes of Purists towards the New Englishes. The voice of the purists is said to have been first uttered by Prator (1968: 459) who openly, and without mincing words, declares his indignation and contempt against the NEs when he maintains that

> ... the heretical tenet I feel I must take exception to is the idea that it is best, in a country where English is not spoken natively but is widely used as the medium of instruction, to set up the local variety of English as the ultimate model to be imitated by those learning the language. (Prator, ibid.)

Prator's (ibid.) declaration invited various reactions from scholars of the other school of thought. These reactions shall be discussed in §1.3.1.

Like Prator, Quirk (1985: 6) holds that the unintelligibility of the NEs necessitates reliance on Standard British English which is a "single monochrome standard form that looks as good on paper as it sounds on speech" (Quirk, ibid.). Quirk's view does not only relegate the NEs to the background, but also excludes American English which has penetrated many parts of the world and even Britain, which is believed to be the traditional seat of mother tongue Englishes.

A view very similar to that of Quirk is expressed by Chevillet (1999: 33) who qualifies the NEs as inferior varieties of English that shouldn't be standardized. He argues that

> Foreigners often wreak havoc on the stress pattern of English polysyllables, they stress personal pronouns which shouldn't be emphasised, and they use strong forms instead of weak forms, thereby jeopardising communication. Should such a state of things be institutionalised or codified? (Chevillet 1999:33)

Chevillet raises a number of issues in the above excerpt which invite some comments. First, who is a "foreigner" in the reasoning of Chevillet? It should be noted that even an American or a Canadian speaker is a foreigner in, say, Britain and Nigeria and vice versa. Second, if we assume that "foreigners", according to Chevillet, refer to speakers of the NEs, then he is in a way perpetuating the dichotomy of "us versus them" – a dichotomy which is very much condemned by those who acknowledge the status of English as a global language. Kachru and Nelson (1996: 79) have cautioned that the dichotomy of "native" and "non-native" speakers or "us versus them" creates attitudinal problems as people are likely to take "non-native" or "foreign" as less worthy "in the sense, for example, that coming in a race is not as good as coming in first" (Kachru and Nelson, ibid.). Third, Chevillet tends to assume that the principal criterion to codify or standardise a variety of a language is the degree of its intelligibility to speakers of other varieties. In fact, among the factors that have been identified in the literature as necessary factors for a variety of a language to be standardised, intelligibility is not even one of them (see, for instance, Bobda's (1994) identification of factors necessary for the standardisation of a variety of a language).

Interestingly, Oji (n. d.), a scholar from an indigenised context, quoted in Jibril (1987: 47), sounding like a single voice in the wilderness, joins the camp of the purists to declare that

> The death-knell of Nigerian English should be sounded *loud and clear* as it has never existed, does not exist now, and will never see the light [sic] of day. (Oji, n. d., quoted in Jibril, 1987: 47)

It should be pointed out that Oji's position as an Outer Circle scholar, as shall be noticed in the next section, is, in fact, a single voice in the wilderness. Many speakers of the New Englishes hold their varieties of English in a very high esteem.

Greenbaum (1990: 22) has also stated that "linguists should promote linguistic variants that have international currency and those that would not lead to misunderstanding in international communication". The same view is expressed by Honey, who insists that "standard English is the form of English which best prepares the student for the challenges encountered in our highly technological and sophisticated society" (Honey 1997: 246)). Modiano (1999: 6) sees Honey as the most aggressive defender of the "integrity" of Standard English whom he considers as a "maverick, someone fighting for a just cause ... [some one] who aims to right a wrong" (Modiano, ibid.).

The views of the purists underscored so for advocate absolute standards in English. They argue that the need for international intelligibility dictates the promotion of only Standard English. But it should be noted that the notion of Standard English itself, as echoed in Modiano (1999: 7), does not have a straight-forward definition, given the current status of the English language in the world where each English-speaking community is claiming its own standard. Literature provides such catchphrases as "Ghanaian Standard English", "Nigerian Standard English" and "American Standard English". It is not surprising that Modiano (ibid.) holds that the "definition of Standard English must be based upon a macro-perspective". This implies that any attempt to define Standard English should consider the current situation of the English language which is gradually acquiring different standards in different areas of the globe.

1.3.2 Attitudes of Pragmatists towards the New Englishes. As thesis and antithesis are dialectical dynamics necessary for a healthy synthesis, the views of the purists could not go without much criticism. In fact, there is a whole school of thought which strongly opposes the views of the purists. Unlike the purists, pragmatists argue for the legitimacy and equality of Englishes in the three concentric circles, stressing that English being an international language, mother speakers cannot continue to be the sole norm setters as if English is their private property. It is in line with this standpoint that Kachru (1986: 103) considers Prator's (1968) attitude as sinful. He accuses Prator of "seven attitudinal sins" and maintains that such a view ignores the inevitable processes of acculturalisation and indigenisation which the English language has undergone in Third World countries (Kachru 1986: 103). He further argues that "the New Englishes have become the unavoidable companion of most, if not all, Outer Circle speakers of English" (Kachru 1986:117). In the same light, Kachru and Nelson (1996:89) argue that

> If a typical American has no wish to speak like or be labelled as a British user of English, why should a Nigerian, an Indian or a Singaporean user feel any differently? (Kachru and Nelson, 1996: 89)

It should be pointed out that, in line with the argument expressed by Kachru and Nelson (ibid.), in most indigenised contexts, the NEs are seen as self-contained systems of communication which are capable of expressing all communication needs. Sey (1973: 1), for example, reports that Ghanaians who attempt to approximate RP are "frowned upon as distasteful" (Sey 1973:1). Some people in Ghana are reported to be so aggressive to the point of suggesting that

> If we can't decide on one Ghanaian language for the country after twenty-nine years of independence, then why shouldn't a borrowed language be *butchered*. (Duodu 1986: 3 quoted in Schmied 1991: 172)

Such a standpoint is rather too extreme and does not reflect the general tendency among Outer Circle speakers. The general attitude of Outer Circle speakers of English is very much in line with the one expressed by Sey (1973). For instance, Mbangwana (1987) also reports that Cameroonians who have traces of any foreign accent in their speech are ridiculed and looked upon as "pedantic been-tos". Bailey and Robinson (1973: 71) testify that "the view that the only suitable model for Indian teachers is British RP is not shared by the vast majority of the people in the country, not even by distinguished teachers of English" (Bailey and Robinson, P.71). Bamgbose (1971: 41) expresses the same view when he maintains that "Many Nigerians will consider as affected or even snobbish any Nigerian who speaks like a native speaker of English" (Bamgbose,

P.41). In fact, in almost every community where a New English is used, the same view is expressed (see, for example, Passé 1947: 53; Leith 1983: 109 and Platt et al. 1984: 388).

Braj Kachru is not the only pragmatist who persuasively defends the integrity, equality, and acceptability of the new varieties of English, though he is graded as the champion of that school of thought. Achebe (1965: 29 f, quoted in Todd 1999:30), expresses a feeling of acceptance of the NEs and the need to promote these local varieties of English when he maintains that

> So my answer to the question 'Can an African ever learn English well enough to be able to use it effectively in creative writing?' is certainly yes. If on the other hand you ask 'can he ever learn to use it as a native speaker?' I should say, I hope not. It is neither necessary nor desirable for him to be able to do so. The price a world language must be prepared to pay is submission to many different kinds of use. (Achebe, 1965: 29f quoted in Todd, 1999: 30)

Achebe's view in the above excerpt goes a long way to enhance the views of the pragmatists—that the NEs are valid and complete systems of communication. Another interesting point suggested by Achebe in the excerpt is the fact that English, being a world language, should be prepared to pay the price of 'submission to many different kinds of use', a wish highly opposed by purists, as underscored in the previous section.

Todd (1999: 30), like other pragmatists, holds that the NEs "keep alive a world view that might otherwise have disappeared" (Todd 1999:30). She argues strongly that "we can lose an entire civilisation when we lose a language". If the NEs have to be downgraded, then she wonders whether "dialect speakers are to be expelled to a place of darkness where they shall be weeping and gnashing of teeth". She shares with Kachru (1986: 103) who maintains that in new ecological contexts "English is used to teach and maintain the indigenous patterns of life and culture, to provide a link in culturally and linguistically pluralistic societies, and to maintain a continuity and uniformity in educational, administrative and legal systems"(Kachru, P.103).

Tripathi (1999: 33) is another scholar who joins the other pragmatists to defend the NEs. In his opinion, "every language has its productivity" (Tripathi 1999:33). He cites Radindranath Tagere, a Nobel Laureate of the colonial period who produced literary works in Bengali and Ngugi Wa Thion'O who has also been publishing in Gikuyu. The implication of this view is that the local varieties of English are capable of serving an important communicative and creative function, in spite of the negative attitudes and perceptions of the purists.

One can notice that among the pragmatists (those who tolerate the local varieties of English), there are quite a good number of Inner Circle speakers. But Bobda (1994:18), after Kachru (1986: 22), categorises the tolerance from mother tongue English speakers into genuine tolerance and one "which is akin to apartheid" (Bobda, ibid.). In the latter, the traditional native speaker tolerates local forms of English as a linguistic means to emphasize the gap that exists between him/her, the colonial master/mistress, and the colonial servant. He shares with Kachru (1986: 22) the view that "the colonisers in their attempt to establish and maintain this [gap] did not insist on teaching their language too well to the colonised Asians or Africans". Bobda (P.18) goes further to cite Christophersen (1973: 83) who puts forth the same view by remarking that for some *Britons*, an Outer Circle who sounds too native-like in his/her speech is intruding into their privacy. To them (the Britons), such an intruding tendency "is as if an uninvited guest had started making free with his host's possession" (Bobda 1994:18, quoting Christophersen 1973: 83). Genuine tolerance, on the other hand, sincerely welcomes the NEs as a historical reality and a phenomenon to be reckoned with. Such a level of tolerance, Bobda (P.18) maintains, is expressed in Platt et al. (1984), Trudgill and Hannah (1985), Todd and Hancock (1986).

In the discussion underscored so far in this section, we have been examining two contrasting schools of thought: those of purists and pragmatists. The former insistently advocates the preservation of purity in the English language and the latter preaches the tolerance and the promotion of local varieties of English. The two schools of thought are championed by two "four stars generals" in English language scholarship: Lord Randolph Quirk and Professor Braj Kachru (Bamgbose 1998:1, quoted in Bobda 2000 c: 54). If we use the logicians' terminologies of "thesis" and "antithesis" to qualify the two schools of thought, then we can easily notice that the discussion is not complete if we do not refer to "synthesis", a third school of thought which reconciles the first and the second schools. In the section that follows, we shall therefore underscore the views of those scholars whose attitudes towards the NEs tend to reconcile advocates of purism and pragmatism, as they acknowledge the inevitability of the NEs, but caution that the linguistic features of these Englishes to be promoted should be those that do not impair international intelligibility.

1.3.3 *Reconciling Purism and Pragmatism.* If we submit the discussion in this section to the war-like tone in Bamgbose (1998:1), quoted in Bobda (2000c: 54), then we shall refer to those scholars who attempt to reconcile purism and pragmatism as peace-makers. Such scholars include Jibril (1987), Crystal (1988), Schmied (1991), Bobda (1999) and Modiano (1999). Their attempts to reconcile the two schools of thought drummed by Lord Randolph Quirk and Professor Kachru and their respective followers take different approaches, as shall be underscored below.

Crystal (1988: 265), for instance, reconciles the two schools when he suggests that

> We may, in due course, all need to be in control of two standard Englishes – the one which gives us our national or local identity, and the one which puts us in touch with the human race. (Crystal 1988: 265)

Crystal's (ibid.) view reconciles the two schools of thought as he recognises the notion of Englishes and at the same time advocates international intelligibility which can guarantee the 'human race' to be in touch with one another. It should be noted that Crystal's (ibid.) proposal is very insightful and pertinent as is likely to relax the muscles of the belligerents of the two camps which are so tensed to the point that only a war-like tone could be used by Bamgbose (1998) to depict the situation.

Jibril (1987: 46f) also recognises the unavoidable existence of Nigerian English, a position which can be extended to all NEs, and the need for international intelligibility to be enhanced. He states his position as follows:

> Nigerian English has developed distinct phonetic, phonological, lexical and syntactic characteristics which are quite stable and which cannot be regarded as deviations from a native norm which Nigerians do not, in any case, aspire to approximate ... Within this school of thought, there are some scholars such as Odumuh (1984) who do not only aggressively assert the existence of Nigerian English but also claim that there is already a standard version of it which we should codify and teach in our schools in place of a foreign grammatical model. This is an extreme position which few people share with Odumuh ... Nigerians will acquire Nigerian English whether or not they are taught in it, so attention is to be focused on supplementing this variety of English with a native-like model in order to enhance the international intelligibility of Nigerians. (Jibril, 1987: 46f)

Jibril's (1987) position, like that of Crystal (1988), recognizes the existence of Nigerian English, but emphasizes the need for international communication.

Another scholar who takes a middle position by acknowledging the existence of local forms of English as forces to be reckoned with and at the same time emphasizing the need for international intelligibility is Schmied (1991). Focusing particularly on the African situation, he maintains that

> Like many other things imported from Europe, such as religious denominations, money economies, legal systems, English is first of all a foreign object, although obviously a necessary one. A modern African society cannot reject a formerly

European, but now international language completely; but it cannot and will not for reasons of practicality as well as of identity, follow the imported model very closely either. (Schmied, 1991)

He goes further to establish that

According to the principle of linguistic autonomy, members of a speech community may choose for themselves which language (or language variety) they want to use. (Schmied, 1991)

But he does not also forget to stress that this principle of linguistic autonomy is possible only when it fosters "communication and understanding between different groups, but not when this creates social barriers" (Schmied, 1991: 209).

A position almost similar to that of Schmied (1991) is that of Bobda (1999: 29). He acknowledges, like other proponents of the local varieties of English, "the urgent need for linguists to hasten the process of description and codification of New Englishes to offer teachers WHAT to teach" (Bobda, 1999), but also emphasizes, like the purists, the need to "teach what is available as norms in current dictionaries and textbooks" (Bobda, 1999).

The last scholar to be considered in this section, who attempts to reconcile the opponents and the proponents of the NEs, is Modiano (1999). Like the pragmatists, he argues that since "non-native speakers outnumber native speakers" (Modiano, 1999:7), the definition of what Standard English is, "directly impacts on the lives of tens of millions of language users in the world" (Modiano, 1999). He further maintains that Standard English should "allow all speakers of the language an equal say in the definition and development of the tongue" (Modiano, ibid: 4). Like the purists, Modiano (ibid:12) maintains that "an inclusion of strong regional accents into the paradigm of standard English is illogical" (Modiano, ibid.). He therefore opts for English as an International language (EIL) , a variety of English, he postulates, "will allow all speakers an equal say in the definition and development of the tongue" and which will be "comprehensible in the international context" (Modiano, ibid.).

From the point of view of practicality, Modiano's EIL involves a number of debatable issues. First, Modiano (P. 12) maintains that "an inclusion of strong regional accents into the paradigm of standard English is illogical" and that EIL should only "include forms of the language that are comprehensible to competent speakers of the language world-wide" (P. 7). But it should be noted that typical features of the NEs are observable even in the speech of university dons and this implies that Modiano's parameter of defining EIL will automatically exclude the NEs. At this point in time, the NEs should logically pose intelligibility problems to speakers of older Englishes, given that such varieties of English are said to be undergoing the processes of acculturalisation and indigenisation (see Kachru 1986). It is not surprising that Bobda (2000c: 60) observes that speakers of older Englishes and those of the NEs will continue to strain their ears to understand each other if they do not make a conscious effort to learn each other's English.

The second debatable issue in Modiano's proposal is the fact he establishes that EIL should be defined from a macro perspective thereby taking into consideration "forms of the language which are considered "correct" by a large number of English-speaking people, whether they be native or non-native speakers" (Modiano, P. 7). Taking such a parameter of defining EIL into consideration, Modiano unwittingly includes all the features of the NEs in the paradigm of EIL. This is because "non-native speakers outnumber native speakers" (Modiano, ibid.: 7) and most non-native speakers see nothing wrong with their varieties of English (see, for instance, Sey 1973, Kachru 1986, Mbangwana 1987 and Awonusi 1989). The last debatable point in Modiano's EIL is quite obvious. If his original intention is to include the NEs in the definition of EIL and EIL is hoped to be intelligible to "competent speakers of the language world-wide" (Modiano, ibid.: 7), then, how does he account for the fact that features of indigenised Englishes which he includes in the paradigm of EIL fail to be intelligible to many mother tongue speakers of English (see, for example, § 1.2 for the numerous cases of intelligibility problems involving mother and 'educated' Outer Circle speakers of English)?

In the discussion so far in §1.3.3, it is underscored that the attitudes of some scholars towards the new varieties of English tend to reconcile advocates of purism and those of pragmatism as they acknowledge the need for the existence of local forms of English, but caution that international intelligibility should not be sacrificed. In taking such a middle position, various proposals are made. For example, Crystal (1988: 265) recommends the promotion of two standard Englishes: the one which gives a speaker his/her national or local identity and the one which puts him/her in touch with the rest of the human race (Crystal, 1988). Modiano on his part advocates English as an international language– a proposal which is highly debatable. Given the different attitudes of scholars towards the NEs, as underscored in the previous sections, what is therefore the status of these local forms of English in the classroom?

1.4 The Status of the New Englishes in the Classroom

The debate concerning the place of the NEs in the classroom is just as hot as that concerning the status of these local forms of English in general. As pointed out in Bobda (2000c: 65), the debate can be perceived in argumentative titles like "The teacher's dilemma" (Platt et al. 1984: ch. 7); "World Englishes: to teach or not to teach?" (Brown 1995) and "Torn between the norms" (Bamgbose 1998). A survey of scholars' opinion on the issue shows a spectrum of views which range from tolerance to views that consider the NEs as "the uninvited guest to be driven out [of the classroom] at all costs" (Bobda 2000:65).

Like the argument expressed against the acceptability of the NEs, Prator (1968) argues that

> If teachers in many different parts of the world aim at the same stable, well documented model, the general effects of their instruction will be convergent; the speech of their pupils will become more and more similar to that of pupils in many other regions, and the area within which communication is possible will grow positively larger. (Prator, 1968)

Prator thinks that the NEs lack stability and sufficient documentation and, for this reason, he thinks they shouldn't be used as a medium of instruction in the classroom. According to him, the promotion of many "diverse models" in the Outer Circle classrooms can only bring about diversity in the speech of the pupils learning the language in different parts of the world. In such a situation, he argues, there can be no hope for international intelligibility.

Prator's view is strictly shared by other purists like Quirk (1985), Honey (1997) and Chevillet (1999). But non-purists rather advocate the teaching and promotion of local varieties of English, which, they believe, are capable of reinforcing the learner's sense of his/her culture. This position is vividly epitomised in a document quoted in Schmied (1991: 178) which was issued by the Zimbabwean Ministry of Education and Culture shortly after independence (precisely in 1982). The document reads thus:

> For Zimbabwe, L2 learning has to be associated more and more with features of the learner's culture and to reject what are considered alien and unacceptable features of the second-language culture-usually to reinforce the individual's sense of his own culture. Methods influenced by such considerations and certainly teaching materials will reflect attitudes towards the desired cultural context of L2 learning. (quoted in Schmied, 1991:178)

The document tends to insist on an indigenised variety of English which is acculturalised with features of the local context. The document sees the insistence on Inner Circle linguistic features in the Outer Circle classrooms to be incompatible with learners whose world-view is deeply rooted in a particular culture.

Schon (1987: 25f), quoted in Bobda (1994: 15), equally argues that it is illogical to insist on Inner Circle English norms in Outer Circle classrooms. She recommends four criteria for choosing a model to be promoted in such contexts. First, the model should be the variety most admired in the students' part of the world. As revealed in §1.3.2, most so-called non-native speakers hold their variety of English in a high esteem. Second, the model should reflect the use the students will make of English. Third, the model should consider the attitude of the school administration. Fourth, the choice of the model should depend on the availability of teaching materials.

Taking a similar position like Schon (1987), Modiano (1999: 6) argues that

> an insistence on near-native proficiency goals in language learning based on BrE model contributes to forces which uphold class differentiation within the communities where such language programs are carried out. (Modiano, 1999)

He further argues that the imposition of a British English-based model on students pursuing English language studies in indigenised contexts is

> A linguistic chauvinism [which] is so deeply rooted, not only in British culture, but also in the minds and hearts of a large number of language teachers working abroad .... [who] find it difficult to accept that other varieties of English, for some learners are better choices for the educational model in the teaching of English as a foreign or second language. (Modiano, ibid.)

Modiano's view is strikingly similar to that of Bamgbose (1971: 41) who maintains that the aim of English language teaching in Outer Circle contexts "is not to produce speakers of British Received Pronunciation" (Bamgbose, 1971) and that of Gimson (1980: 303) who considers it 'a mistake' to rely on Inner Circle norms in Outer Circle classrooms.

In spite of the strong arguments put forth by pragmatists, the teaching of the NEs is still to become a complete reality. According to Bobda (2000c: 66), the difficulty of teaching the NEs in indigenised contexts is accounted for by two main reasons. First, the NEs are not yet codified and, as a consequence, tend to have no relevant didactic materials. Second, he maintains that there are limited professional and educational opportunities attached to features of the NEs "in a world almost exclusively controlled by the West" (Bobda, 2000c:66). He however predicts a possible development in the 21st century where "there would be the appearance of dictionaries and grammars of national Englishes like Cameroon / Nigerian / Tanzanian / Malaysian English, or of regional Englishes like West African English, East African English, South Asian English and so on" (Bobda, 2000c).

The discussion so far in this chapter can be recapitulated by re-asserting that the NEs display linguistic peculiarities which are significantly different from those of older Englishes and, as a result, there are bound to be serious intelligibility problems between Inner Circle and Outer Circle English speakers. The inevitable consequence of these intelligibility problems is the expression of different attitudes and reactions. These reactions and attitudes "form a spectrum which varies from hilarious attitudinal epithets to a plea for linguistic tolerance" (Kachru 1986: 100). In the light of this spectrum of reactions and attitudes, one cannot hesitate to join Bobda (2000c: 65) in asking the question: "Do the new Englishes have a place in the ELT classroom other than that of the uninvited guest to be driven out [of the classroom] at all costs?" (Bobda, ibid)

1.5 A Focus on Cameroon English

Cameroon English has been diligently studied by prominent Cameroonian researchers such as Masanga (1983), Mbangwana (1987), Bobda (1994), Chumbow and Bobda (1996) and Kouega (1991). Before making a brief survey of these studies, as a necessary prerequisite to draw the dichotomy between the present investigation and previous ones (see §2.7), it is imperative to first of all provide a historico-sociolinguistic landscape of Cameroon.

1.5.1 A Historico-sociolinguistic Landscape of Cameroon. The historical and sociolinguistic landscape of Cameroon is revealed in Mbassi-Manga (1973), Todd (1991) and Chumbow and Bobda (1996). The Portuguese are reported to have been the first European settlers to discover Cameroon in 1472. The heavy multilingual nature of the country made them to rely, at first, on African translators to break through communication problems (Todd 1991:1), but later on, a pidginised Portuguese was developed.

After the discovery of the country by the Portuguese, other Europeans like the Dutch, the Swedes, the Danes, the Spaniards, the Germans, the French, the British and the Poles have lived in Cameroon at different historical points for various reasons. These reasons range from commercial, educational, religious to political reasons. Commercially, the settlers showed great interest in slave trade up to the 19th century. Todd (ibid.), after Mbassi–Manga (1973), reveals that West Africa was often referred to as the 'slave Coast' because European traders actually traded in human beings. They were also interested in the trading of food, ivory and gold. This is testified in the use of expressions such as "Grain Coast", "Rio dos Camerones", the "Ivory Coast" and the "Gold Coast" (see Todd, 1991 and Chumbow and Bobda 1996: 43).

Religiously and educationally, the European settlers had the tasks of evangelising and educating the indigenous Cameroonian population. A number of mission schools were opened to promote Western Education and Christianity. Protestant missionaries were most active in promoting religious activities.

Chumbow and Bobda (ibid.) reveal that by the end of the 18th century, the British dominated the other Europeans on the Cameroonian coast in terms of their commercial, religious, educational and political activities. The linguistic consequence of the dominance of British influence on the West African coast in general and in Cameroon in particular was the gradual replacement of a Portuguese-based Pidgin by English and Pidgin English. The British are said to have had a very cordial relationship with the local chiefs and Kings and this can be seen in the invitation extended to Queen Victoria of Britain by these local leaders for the annexation of Cameroon. Due to the sluggish attitude of the British government to respond to the request, a German envoy, Dr. Gustav Nachtigal, went ahead and signed a treaty with Kings Bell and Akwa in July 12, 1884, thereby annexing Cameroon as a German protectorate. This was symbolised by the hoisting of the German flag on the right bank of river Wouri (Chumbow and Bobda, ibid., after Zé Amvela, 1993).

During the German rule, though German was declared as the official language, English and Pidgin English were still widely used, complemented by the use of the local languages by the indigenous population. The Germans continued to administer Cameroon as a German protectorate until 1918 when Germany was defeated in the First World War. At the treaty of Versailles, Cameroon was seized from Germany and partitioned between Britain and France to be governed as "British Cameroons" and "French Cameroons" under the League of Nations Mandate. Following the collapse of the League of Nations and the creation of the United Nations, the two Cameroons were placed under the United Nations Trusteeship (Chumbow and Bobda, 1996).

On January 1, 1960, the French Cameroons was granted self-government. On February 12, 1961, the British Cameroons which Britain was administering as part of Nigeria, was submitted to a plebiscite to choose whether to remain as part Nigeria or to reunite with the newly independent Republic of Cameroon or the former French Cameroons. The northern portion of British Cameroons opted to join Nigeria while the southern part chose to unite with the independent Republic of Cameroon. On October 1, 1961, the independent French-speaking Republic of Cameroon and Southern Cameroons became the Federal Republic of Cameroon. Each federated state exercised a certain degree of autonomy in education, administration and the legal system (Chumbow and Bobda, ibid.). In 1972, the two states merged into the United Republic of

Cameroon, with English and French becoming the two official languages of the country. It was not until 1984 when the National Assembly voted a law which changed the name of the country to "Republic of Cameroon", the name of the former 'French Cameroon'. It is pointed out in Chumbow and Bobda (ibid.) that such a move has been seen by the Anglophones as an attempt by the majority group (Francophones) to assimilate the minority who are the Anglophones.

Given the historical evolution of the country, a complex linguistic landscape is inevitable. Today, English is in competition with a multitude of languages in Cameroon. The competition from French is very obvious, given that English shares most of its official functions with French. Pidgin English is equally reported in Koenig et al. (1983) and re-echoed in Chumbow and Bobda (1996) to be the most widely spoken language in Cameroon. But its functions do not significantly intrude into that of English. English is regarded as the language of official transactions whereas Pidgin English, though very widely used, remains the language of intimacy and informal transactions. Besides the challenge from French and Pidgin English, English also significantly competes with more than 280 local languages. From the above discussion, it can therefore be seen that Cameroon has an interesting historico-sociolinguistic landscape. The landscape is expected to serve as a necessary background to the understanding of some research statements made on the phonology of CamE which will be our preoccupation in the next section.

1.5.2 Previous Statements on Cameroon English Phonology. A number of illuminating investigations have been carried out on Cameroon English phonology. The most salient ones include Masanga (1983), Bobda (1994), Mbangwana (1987), Kouega (1991), Njoke (1996) and Ngefac (1997). Masanga (1983), for instance, focused his study on the speech of 'educated' Moghamo speakers of English whom he considered to be speakers of Cameroon Standard English. The investigation revealed some segmental aspects of Cameroon English phonology which are, in fact, observable in most NEs, as pointed out in §1.1. Some of the segmental peculiarities of CamE phonology reported by Masanga (1983: 131f) include the simplification of consonant clusters, the monophthongization of diphthongs, divorcing, and so on. Most of these phonological processes are also reported in Mbangwana (1987), Kouega (1991) and Bobda (1994).

It should be noted that Kouega (1991) and Bobda (1994), besides focusing on segmental phonology, examined some supra-segmental aspects of Cameroon English phonology. Kouega, for example, shows how Cameroon English phonology deviates from Standard British English through such aspects as pitch, voice and tone. Bobda (1994), on the other hand, does not only show

how, at the supra-segmental level, stress placement in CamE contrasts with that of RP, but also gives a generative colouring to this variety of English. In fact, he establishes the degree of predictability of segmental and supra-segmental features of Cameroon English phonology by introducing the concept of trilateral process. He defines the concept as a phenomenon whereby a given underlying segment A̲ is restructured to a new underlying form B̲ in a New English: A and B undergo independent phonological processes and surface as A' and B' respectively (For details of this concept, see Bobda 1994, 2000a and b).

Another insightful study on CamE phonology is that of Njoke (1996). Instead of studying CamE phonology in terms of how it deviates from Inner Circle Englishes, as is the case with most studies on this variety of English, Njoke (1996) studied CamE phonology in terms of the diversity that can be observed at the segmental level. He reported that as many as four different pronunciations could be identified for a single word. For example, he revealed that the word "public", for instance, was pronounced by his informants either as /pɔblik/, /pɔplik/, /pəbik/ or /pʌbllik/. He correlated this diversity with some categories of speakers like media professionals, university teachers of English, students and clergymen.

CamE phonology has equally been studied by Ngefac (1997) in terms of how some sociolinguistic variables correlate with phonological variables (see §2.1.3.2 for some highlights of this investigation).

Chapter Two
A Critical Review of Previous Sociolinguistic Patterns

2. Introduction

As demonstrated in the last chapter, in the new settings where the English language has been transplanted, distinctive linguistic peculiarities have emerged and these peculiarities are conditioned by the historical, ecological, sociolinguistic and cultural realities of these new contexts. Given that the realities of the Western world are significantly different from those of New English contexts, a critique of previously reported sociolinguistic patterns between linguistic variables and the different social categories (e.g. social class, gender, age and ethnicity) would be made as an attempt to eventually assess whether the same patterns of correlation are likely to prevail in a new ecological setting, such as Cameroon, where English is not used as a mother tongue.

As the literature shows, studies of different magnitudes have been carried out in many Western English contexts to establish how language is a reflection of social categories or to reveal what Chomsky (1980: 24-5), after Putnam (n. d.), refers to as the "social division of linguistic labor". These studies (e.g. Fischer 1958; Labov 1966, 1972; Trudgill 1972, 1974 and Macaulay 1976, 1977) tend to be largely unanimous in establishing certain correlation patterns between some sociolinguistic variables and linguistic variables. A critique of these correlation patterns would be the major preoccupation of this chapter.

2.1 The Correlation between Social Class and Linguistic Variables

Despite Hubbell's (1950) conclusion that New York "was the site of massive free variation" (Chambers 1995: 16), William Labov, a famous American sociolinguist, persuasively established in his 1966 investigation that the social stratification of New York City is significantly reflected in the choice of linguistic variants. Hubbell (1950) has actually concluded in an earlier study of New York community that

> The pronunciation of a large number of New Yorkers exhibits a pattern ... that might most accurately be described as the complete absence of any pattern. Such speakers sometimes pronounce /r/ before a consonant or a pause and sometimes omit it, in a thoroughly haphazard pattern. (Hubbell 1950, quoted in Chambers 1985: 16)

In spite of such an impressionistic conclusion about New York City, Labov (1966) took the bull by the horns and embarked on a study of the same community that has been described as "patternless". One may guess that Labov's inspiration came from Sapir's (1929) insightful statement that

> Behind the lawlessness of social phenomena there is a regularity of configuration and tendency which is just as real as the regularity of physical processes in the mechanical world. (Sapir 1929)

The major point of interest here is not where Labov got his inspiration. The important point is how Labov successfully contradicted facts previously established by his predecessor about the New York City. William Labov, accompanied by one field assistant, Michael Kac, engaged in the study of the city of New York. A total of 157 informants and 58 children of the informants were interviewed. These informants were selected from different ethnic groups, age levels and social classes (Chambers 1995). They were submitted to the reading of pre-prepared texts in different phonological styles.

2.1.1 Labov and the Problem of Observer's Paradox.

But how did Labov avoid distorting the very facts he set out to collect? This question introduces us to the fundamental sociolinguistic problem of *observer's paradox*. Labov himself states that "the aim of linguistic research in the community must be to find out how people talk when they are not systematically observed; yet we can only obtain this data by systematic observation" (Labov 1970: 32). The implication of this statement is that true and natural sociolinguistic data should be obtained from informants using a method that does not distort the results. The problem of observer's paradox in other words refers to the tendency whereby research subjects sound unnatural simply because they know they are being monitored or observed. Chambers (1995:19) compares the problem to Murray's (1985) "Hawthorne effect", a similar problem in the social sciences whereby the behaviour of experimental subjects tend to change simply because they perceive themselves as participants in the experiment (Chambers 1995).

Labov actually used different strategies to ensure that the data he set out to collect were natural and undistorted. He gradually introduced topics that aroused the subjects' emotions and this made them to be "caught up in the recollected urgency of the situation" (Chambers 1995: 6). Another strategy he used to overcome this problem was creating a situation whereby family members and friends frequently stepped in to interrupt the discussions. This gave an opportunity for the subjects' attention to be diverted while the tape recorder was turned on. As one would expect, free-flowing and natural speech was recorded from the informants.

However, according to Baugh (1993: 178), honesty to the informants is the most appropriate way to register true and natural speech. He argues that when informants are made to know their role in linguistic research, they are likely to speak naturally. He maintains that in a situation where informants do not know their role, they are bound to be suspicious and, in such a situation, they cannot speak freely. He argues that

> The extent to which informants tend to ignore recording equipment in favour of speaking freely is a direct reflection of the extent to which field workers have successfully overcome the observer's paradox. (Baugh 1993: 179)

He goes further to state as follows:

> I always told informants about my work; there has been no need to hide my interest in language or culture, as well as in the people who preserve them. Honesty may lead to the kind of rapport that can overcome the observer's paradox .(Baugh, 1993:179)

Whatever suggestion Baugh may be making does not cancel the fact that the two authors recognise the need for natural and free-flowing data, but they differ on the way this natural data should be obtained. It should however be pointed out that, although the problem of observer's paradox is unanimously acknowledged as fundamental in any sociolinguistic study, a researcher's sensitivity to it all depends on the nature of data intended to be collected. A researcher who intends to collect data in a formal style, for instance, should not be concerned at all with the problem. After all, the expectations of a formal context warrant the informants to be conscious that they all being monitored so that they can set their speech consciousness nerves at work. Labov (1966) needed to be very sensitive to the problem of observer's paradox because he intended to collect data in a casual context where subjects are normally expected to be natural in their speech. The degree to which Labov succeeded in overcoming the problem can be seen in the significant correlation that emerged from his New York study.

2.1.2 The Stratification of the Post-vocalic /r/ in New York. Labov's investigation involved many phonological variables, but the one which yielded the most impressive results involved the degree of occurrence of the post vocalic /r/ in words such as "car", "floor" and "fourth". The study revealed a number of interesting findings. The general observation he established is that "there are linguistic hierarchies which correspond to social hierarchies, and the persons with highest status of greatest potential for exercising power are always speakers of the linguistic variety which is judged to be the most logical,

beautiful and comprehensible" (Milroy and Milroy 1985:110). It was, in fact, discovered that the use of prestige and stigmatized linguistic features was significantly graded according to the social status of the speakers and according to the phonological style under which the speakers' speech was realised. He pointed out that only the UMC used the prestigious /r/ in less formal styles with some degree of consistency and that the LMC usage in the more formal styles surpassed that of the UMC, a situation he associated with the phenomenon of "hypercorrection". Bobda and Mbangwana (1993:184) define the notion of hyper-correction as "the phenomenon whereby users of substandard or stigmatised language feature attempt to use the standard or prestigious feature and in the process, 'go farther' than required". Labov explained that the LMC tended to hyper-correct because of their sensitivity to social pressures since their social position is on the borderline between the middle and the working class. Their social position therefore made them feel insecure. It is as a result of this insecurity that the LMC had the strong endeavour to sound more correct, prestigious and refined than the class above them. This pattern which emerged from the study of the New York City led Labov to establish the famous (1966) sociolinguistic report.

2.1.3 The Labovian 1966 Sociolinguistic Report. Whether Labov's (1966) sociolinguistic finding is appreciated as a theory or simply as a sociolinguistic report, the obvious fact is that his findings remain a major sociolinguistic discovery and that explains why 40 years after the study, similar studies can still be conveniently carried out in different communities. What is particularly interesting is that in a community that was previously described as displaying no predictable correlation pattern between linguistic variables and social hierarchy (see Hubbell 1950), Labov (1966) successfully established that there was, indeed, a significant correlation. He unambiguously established that as one moves up the social ladder, the rate of occurrence of prestige forms of speech also increases (see, for instance, the case of /r/) and vice versa. In appreciation of such a discovery, scholars from different parts of the world have immortalised William Labov in different ways. Chambers (1995:15), for instance, says Labov has "inspired other linguists to head into the streets with notepads in their hands and tape recorders over their shoulders". Jibril (1982:290) on his part remarks that Labov has elevated sociolinguistics from "mere impressionism to scientific replicability" (Jibril 1982:290) and one can add that Labov is one of the pioneer fathers of modern sociolinguistics. Similar studies have been carried out in other Western contexts and the results unambiguously confirm Labov's 1966 report. In Norwich, Trudgill's (1974) investigation of the linguistic variable /ɑ:/ (the standard English vowel in words like *after, path, cart*, etc.) revealed that the deviant variant /a:/ characterized the speech of WC groups and the prestige variant was more observable in the speech of the MC groups.

A similar pattern has equally been established in Glasgow. Macaulay (1976) stratified his Glaswegian subjects into the following classes:

Class I - professionals and managers

Class II a - White-collar, intermediate non-manual workers

Class II b - skilled manual

Class III - semi-skilled and unskilled manual workers

In Macaulay's investigation, the expected pattern emerged, thereby confirming Labov's (1966) findings and those of related studies. He noticed a significant correlation between his phonological variables and the social class of his subjects. The correlation pattern obtained from studies similar to Labov's (1966) New York study is an indication that the Labovian discovery should be acclaimed a theory, even if his goal was not to establish one.

2.1.4 *The Applicability of the Labovian Report in a New English Context.*

The socio-political and sociolinguistic realities of some of the New English contexts, especially those of Africa, would be used to assess the applicability of the Labovian report in such contexts. It should be noted right from the outset that in most European countries and the United States, the model of social class upon which Labov's investigation was based neatly reflects the social structure, but this contrasts with the situation of most African countries and other non-industrialised English contexts, which do not have well-defined models of social structure that describe the social structure, as shall be explained later. Interestingly, in the Western world class distinction is so obvious to the extent that it is considered abnormal when one steps out of his/her class to interact meaningfully with individuals from other classes (Chambers 1995:48). According to Chambers, there are "some social pressures that keep people in their place" (Chambers ibid.). The question of what actually determines a speaker's social class is inevitable. According to Chambers (ibid.:43), "occupation is the touchstone of social class membership". In the following table, he attempts to correlate the social classes with the different occupational groups in industrialised societies.

Table 2a: Social classes in correlation with occupational status

Middle Class(MC)	- Upper Middle Class (UMC): owners, directors, people with inherited wealth - Middle Middle Class (MMC): Professionals, executive managers - Lower Middle Class (LMC): Semi- professionals, lower managers
Working Class (WC)	- Upper Working Class (UWC): Clerks, skilled manual workers - Middle Working Class (MWC): semi-skilled manual workers - Lower Working Class: Unskilled labourers, seasonal workers

(Chambers 1995:37)

As can be noticed from the table, in industrialised societies the notion of social class is principally a function of occupation, though there are other minor factors that are also considered. The stratification of society in Western contexts is based actually on "whether one earns a living by working with his/her hands or by pencil-work and services" (Chambers, 1995). In America, the middle class and the working class are referred to as "white-collar workers" and "blue-collar workers" respectively. Chambers (ibid.) points out that the metaphors of "white-collar" and "blue-collar" reflect "the conventional workplace attire of white shirt-and-tie or open-necked blue denim" (Chambers, ibid.). He argues that, although the metaphors of "white-collar" and "blue-collar" coincide with middle class groups and working class groups respectively, they do not perfectly fit the schema illustrated in the table above. This is illustrated by the fact that clerical workers classified under UWC in the table are physically seen as white-collar workers because of their usual dignified attire, but they are, in actual fact, blue-collar workers because of their occupational status. Another illustration is the fact that blue-collar plumbers, electricians, and cabinet markers "who rise through the ranks to take on duties as supervisors and overseers are generally LMC, though their attire may not be different from the workers in their crews" (Chambers, ibid.:38).

But in New English contexts, especially African countries, the notion of social class is quite foreign. In fact, such expressions as Upper Middle Class, Middle Middle Class, Upper Working Class, Middle Working Class and Lower Working Class are not often used to qualify speakers with different social statuses. Instead, we seem to have what is referred to in Jibril's (1982) study as socio-economic groupings – a pyramid-based social structure that identifies the residual mass at the bottom of the pyramid; the sub-elite at the middle of the pyramid and the elite at the top of the pyramid. But it should be noted that such a pyramid-based model of social structure does not equally provide clear-cut parameters that should be considered to place speakers at the different rungs of the social ladder. A model of social structure that realistically reflects the realities of most African countries should not consider occupational status as the touchstone upon which the model is based, as is the case with the social class structure (which is, anyway, wonderfully convincing in the Western world) upon which Labov's study was based. As a further remark, wealth should not also be considered as a major determinant in the construction of such a model, especially if the model is expected to have a significant correlation with linguistic variables.

A number of reasons account for such a position. First, most African countries are characterized by nepotism, (military) dictatorship and favouritism; if at all the list of the vices can be exhausted. In such an atmosphere, there is a high tendency for people to find themselves in very high positions, such as, Directors, Ministers and Managers of big corporations when they do not have the necessary educational background to be in those positions. Their being in such positions of power is merely a function of the type of relationship they share with decision-makers. In most cases, admission into any respectful position like that of a manager of a corporation depends either on whether one is a cousin or brother of a decision-maker or on whether one is an active militant of the political party of the decision-maker. In such a situation where occupational status is not a function of educational attainment, there can be no hope to obtain any significant correlation between English linguistic variables and a social structure that is based on the occupation of the speakers.

Second, it is common to find people in most African countries with very high educational qualifications who are jobless or are involved only in meagre jobs that do not reflect their high educational attainment. This may be as a result of the fact that they do not have god-fathers, as is often said, who can facilitate their attempts to obtain jobs that match with their educational background. As a result, they involve themselves in all types of meagre jobs one can imagine. Using occupational status to stratify such people, they will not have any social status better than that of LWC blue-collar workers, such as, plumbers, electricians, and cabinet-makers. In any attempt to correlate the English linguistic features of such people who have attained a high level of education, but "earn a living by working with the hand and not by pencil-work services" (Chambers 1995), a pattern very different from the one reported in the Western world is likely to be obtained.

Wealth, like occupation, is equally considered a non-essential factor in the construction of a model of social structure that is expected to correlate significantly with English linguistic variables in New English contexts, especially in African countries which do not have the realities of the Western world. Interestingly, there is a massive presence in most African communities of what one may adequately describe as ambiguous individuals. These people refer to rich illiterates whose financial status places them comfortably on the chairs of people with a high social position, but who are at the same time deprived of certain privileges because of their English linguistic deficiency. If such people are placed on the top of the pyramid or classified as Upper Middle Class because of their wealth, one will obviously obtain no significant correlation between their social position and their English linguistic potentials.

One can therefore maintain that the applicability of any sociolinguistic theory in a given context depends significantly on its compatibility with the socio-cultural realities of the place. A place like India, for instance, has a social structure that is neither similar to what is obtained in the Western world nor similar to what is assumed in Jibril (1982) to be a model of social structure for African countries. India rather has what is referred to in the literature as "castes". According to Littlejohn (1972) and Trudgill (1974), castes are stable, clearly defined groups and membership to each caste is said to be hereditary.

The sociolinguistic realities of most New English contexts in general and those of Cameroon in particular equally make it difficult for the type of significant correlation reported in Labov's study to be observable in such contexts. In Cameroon, for instance, besides English and French as the two official languages of the country, there are over 280 indigenous languages, an elaborated Pidgin, known as Kamtok, and a newly created language, known as "Camfranglais", a concoction of most of the languages spoken in Cameroon, observed mostly in the speech of the youths in French-speaking cities, such as Yaounde, Douala, Nkongsamba and Bafoussam. In spite of this complex linguistic landscape, British English and, sometimes, RP are often the target in the ELT industry in Cameroon. If Western English standards should be the goal in the ELT in Cameroon, is it possible that Cameroonian informants can show the same level of competence as Labov's (1966) informants?

After arguing that the sociocultural and sociolinguistic realities of New English contexts make it difficult for the Labovian discovery to be observable in such communities, let's turn our attention to a practical attempt that has been made in Cameroon to carry out an investigation similar to the Labovian study. In earlier investigations (Ngefac 1997 & 2006), an attempt was made to conduct a similar investigation in Cameroon, a New English context. The speech of some Anglophone students in some schools in Yaounde was thoroughly studied. The 30 informants who made up the sample were categorised into high status speakers (HSs) and low status speakers (LSs). HSs and LSs correspond fairly to Labov's MC and WC groups respectively. The categorisation of the subjects into the two groups depended on such factors as the occupation and the place of residence of the parents of the subjects. As concerns occupation, a higher status was attributed to children of top-ranking politicians, directors of big corporations, managers of big firms and other top-ranking civil servants who occupied influential positions. On the other hand, children of not well to do parents who were either farmers in their respective villages or were involved only in meagre jobs in towns were associated with low status. As concerns the place of residence of the parents of the subjects, a residential quarter, such as, Bastos (a quarter highly respected in Yaounde) was assumed to be the quarter of socially superior citizens and Briquetterie (a quarter assumed to be inhabited by the residual mass) was associated with the so-called LSs.

The subjects from the two social groups were submitted to the reading of a series of carefully designed sentences containing 48 targeted English phonological variables. The following table presents the results obtained from the two pseudo-social groups.

Table2b : Pseudo social classes correlating with linguistic variables

	HSs	LSs
Item	% of SBE variants	% of SBE variants
Colonel /ɜː/	0	0
Maximum /ks/	0	0
Country /ʌ/	13.33	20
President /z/	0	6.66
Mayor /ɛə/	0	0
Women /ɪ/	0	0
Maternity /ɜː/	26.66	20
Chair /ɛə/	0	6.66
Calm /ɑː/	0	0
Debt /ø/	6.66	13.33

(Adapted from Ngefac 1997: table 6)

The underlined portions of the words in the table above represent areas that usually pose articulatory problems to Cameroonian speakers of English. The pattern displayed in the table is fairly self-explanatory. None of the pseudo-social groups showed any striking advantage over the other group in the articulation of the SBE variants of the underlined segments of the words. Interestingly, LSs, the group assumed to be socially inferior, appear to have an edge over the group at the other end of the social continuum in the articulation of some of the linguistic items. This advantage, which appears to characterize the speech of LSs, is, however, not very striking. On the whole, there was no substantial correlation between the two social groups and their English linguistic output. The absence of any striking correlation between English linguistic variables and a social structure constructed according to the social class structure upon which Labov's investigation was based further shows that the socio-cultural and sociolinguistic realities of New English contexts make it difficult for similar results to be obtained in Cameroon.

2.1.5 *Constructing a Model of Social Structure for Cameroon.* If a speaker's occupation is judged to be inadequate in the construction of a model of social structure in a place like Cameroon, to what extent can a speaker's level of education, which fairly correlates with linguistic variables, as demonstrated in Chapter Four, be used in the construction of such a model? But it should be noted that under certain circumstances, a speaker's occupation (which is previously argued in this work to be an unreliable factor in the construction of a model of social structure for Cameroon) can at least serve as a sub-criterion in the construction of such a model. If a speaker's occupation has been judged to be an unreliable factor, it is because there is a high tendency in most New English contexts for people to find themselves in certain jobs or in certain positions of power (e.g. Director of a corporation) simply because of their relationship with decision-makers. But in a situation where a speaker's occupation actually matches with his or her level of education, there is every reason to consider both educational attainment and occupational status in the construction of a social structure for Cameroon.

In order to construct such a model of social structure which is expected to reflect the realities of Cameroon and which is equally expected to correlate remarkably with linguistic variables, one cannot claim to have no inspiration from previous models. The notion of social class, for instance, is quite foreign in a New English context, such as, Cameroon, but it provides the framework upon which a different model can be constructed. It is true that in the social class system such expressions as "middle class" and "working class" are quite confusing, but the model at least offers a reliable hint that society is vertically structured into different sub-strata. The pyramid-based model, discussed in Jibril (1982), which identifies the residual mass at the bottom of the pyramid, the sub-elite at the middle of the pyramid and the elite at the top of the pyramid, is judged inadequate in depicting the social structure of most African countries, but it at least confirms that social stratification also exists in African contexts, though it does not clearly state what determines that stratification.

A social structure we wish to propose in this work and which is expected to reflect the Cameroonian reality relies principally on a speaker's level of education and, to an extent, on the Cameroonian Civil Service structure. It is worth revealing at this point that the Civil Service of Cameroon categorises its workers into the following:

- Category A2 Workers: These are generally workers who have at least a Bachelor's degree or its equivalent and who have been trained in a professional school for two years. In some cases, this category of workers may have only the General Certificate of Education (GCE) Advanced Level, a *Baccalauréat* (for Francophones) or an equivalent but must have undertaken a professional training for a period ranging from five to seven years. They always graduate from such a professional school with a postgraduate diploma. It is worth noting that in very rare cases, this category of workers may have simply risen from the last ranks or grades through hard work and longevity.

- Category A1 Workers: This category of workers refers to those whose minimum qualification is the GCE Advanced Level (or Baccalauréat for Francophones) or any equivalent certificate and who have undertaken a professional training for three years. There are equally cases where Category A1 Workers may have access to a professional school with a First Degree qualification, but in this case, the training is less than three years. In some cases, though not very common, Category A1 Workers simply move up from the last ranks.

- Category B2 and Category B1 Workers may all have the GCE Advanced Level or the Baccalauréat as their minimum qualification, but may differ in the number of years they undergo a professional training. There are professional schools from which holders of the GCE Advanced Level or the Baccalauréat certificate graduate as Category B1 Workers after training for nine months or one year, and as Category B2 Workers after training for two years. There is equally the possibility of having simply risen from the last grade through hard work and longevity.

- Category C Workers are those who have the GCE Ordinary Level certificate or the BEPC or any equivalent certificate and who have been trained in a professional school for a period ranging from nine months to one year.

- Category D Workers refer to those whose level of education is the First school Leaving Certificate (FSLC) or the *CEPE* for Francophones and have undergone a professional training of period ranging from three months to one year.

It should be pointed out that, besides the above categories of workers who are generally known in Cameroon as civil servants, the Public Service of Cameroon equally has other types of workers known as state agents and contract workers. In most cases, they do not undertake any professional training like civil servants before being recruited. They are graded in terms of index and a worker's index depends on his or her level of education and longevity. Through the index of these workers, one can easily predict which category in the civil service they are likely to belong to, if they were civil servants.

Having exposed the civil service structure of Cameroon, we shall now go further to establish a social structure that relies mainly on a person's level of education and, to an extent, on his or her occupational status. Such a structure can be schematised as follows:

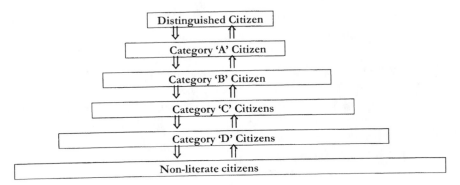

Figure 1: A proposed model of social structure for Cameroon

As shown in the schema above, an attempt has been made to segment the Cameroonian society into six hierarchically different social ranks: distinguished citizen, category 'A' citizen, category 'B' citizen, category 'C' citizen, category 'D' citizen and non-literate citizen. The arrows on the left hand side of the schema present the social ranks in descending order of status and those on the right hand side present them in ascending order. The social rank with the highest status is the distinguished citizen. In order to be considered a distinguished citizen, one needs to have a terminal degree, such as a doctoral degree or an equivalent. One may be a Director, a Manager of a corporation, a military officer and so on and may not qualify as a distinguished citizen if he or she has no doctoral degree or an equivalent certificate. Similarly, a person's wealth does not qualify him or her to be a distinguished citizen if he or she does not have the expected academic qualification. But a rich businessperson who has no job other than his /her business unit, and who has a doctoral degree or an equivalent can conveniently be considered a distinguished citizen. In the same light, a person who has no job at all, or is simply involved in meagre jobs that do not match with his or her qualification, may still enjoy the status of a distinguished if he or she has a doctoral degree or an equivalent. In this case, one can either be privileged or a deprived distinguished citizen. The former is one whose occupational status reflects his or her level of education and the latter is one who has no job at all, or is involved only in meagre jobs, in spite of a level of education that qualifies him or her as a distinguished citizen.

The next social rank, in descending order of status, is referred to as category 'A' citizen. To be a category 'A' citizen, one is expected to have a minimum of a Bachelor's degree or an equivalent. Like the case of a distinguished citizen, one can either be a privileged or a deprived category 'A' citizen, depending on whether his or her occupational status reflects educational attainment. All the workers classified in the civil service of Cameroon as categories A1 and A2 workers and who have a minimum of a First Degree or an equivalent are privileged category 'A' citizens and those who have a minimum of a First Degree and are jobless are deprived category 'A' citizens.

Category 'B' citizen is the next social rank after that of a category 'A' citizen. To be classified as a category 'B' citizen, one needs to have a minimum of a GCE Advanced Level, a Baccalauréat (for French-speaking Cameroonians) or an equivalent. One can either be a privileged category 'B' citizen (if he or she is involved in a job that matches with his or her level of education) or a deprived category 'B' citizen (if the level of education is not reflected in his or her job). Cameroonian civil servants who are classified as categories B1 and B2 workers and who have a minimum of the GCE Advanced Level or a Baccalauréat or an equivalent are necessarily privileged category 'B' citizens. Those who have the GCE Advanced Level or a Baccalauréat or an equivalent and do not have any job at all, or are involved only in meagre jobs that do not reflect their level of education, are deprived category 'B' citizens.

In descending order of status, the social rank after that of category 'B' citizen is that of category 'C' citizen. The minimum qualification for one to have the status of a category 'C' citizen is the GCE Ordinary Level or the BEPC (for French-speaking Cameroonians) or an equivalent. Cameroonian civil servants who are classified as category 'C' workers and who have the GCE Ordinary Level, the BEPC or an equivalent are privileged category 'C' citizens. Those who have the same qualification, but are jobless are deprived category 'C' citizens.

The next social ranks include category 'D' citizen and non-literate citizen. The academic qualification necessary to have the rank of a category 'D' citizen is the First School Leaving Certificate (for Anglophobes) and CEPE (for Francophones). Like the social ranks presented above, one can either be a privileged or a deprived category 'D' citizen, depending on whether his or her level of education is reflected in his or her job. The hierarchically lowest social rank considered in this model is referred to as non-literate citizen. One can have this social rank if he or she has never received any formal education.

What makes this model of social structure different from previous models is the way each of the social ranks is defined. In the social class system, one's occupation is the main factor to determine his or her social class. But in the model underscored above, level of education is the principal criterion to determine a person's social rank. One's occupation only determines whether he or she is a privileged or a deprived citizen of the social rank determined by his or her level of education. In the same light, a person with a certain occupational status, say, a Director, is not necessarily a distinguished citizen in the context of this model, if he or she does not have the expected educational qualification. If such a person with a very high occupational status simply has the GCE

Advanced level or any equivalent certificate, he or she is seen from the context of this model as a category 'B' citizen, irrespective of his or her high occupational position.

It should be emphasised that the model of social structure proposed in this study is simply intended to establish the type of social structure that can correlate significantly with linguistic variables; it is not aimed at promoting class discrimination. With such a model of social structure, which relies mainly on educational attainment, future Cameroonian researchers can embark on similar investigations to establish the correlation between a speaker's social status and linguistic variables. If Ngefac's (2006) study did not succeed in establishing any striking correlation between a speaker's social status and linguistic variables, it is because the investigation relied on the Western world's model of social structure, though it was a conscious attempt to test the workability of such a model in a context like Cameroon. Without a model of social structure, like the one proposed in this study, which reflects the social realities of Cameroon, any investigation to establish the correlation between a speaker's social status and linguistic variables may not yield any significant results. This justifies why this study did not include a speaker's social status in the scope of its investigation, given that such a model which reflects the Cameroonian reality had not existed before. It should equally be pointed out that if Cameroonians welcome the model of social structure proposed in this study as a model that realistically reflects the Cameroonian context, the study of the correlation between a speaker's social status and linguistic variables is likely to yield significant results. In such a situation, Labov's (1966) famous sociolinguistic report is likely to transcend the frontiers of Cameroon and that of any other new English context which finds the model as a good candidate for their community.

It should equally be acknowledged that so long as a SBE accent or any Western English accent continues to be the target, the type of significant correlation between linguistic variables and social status reported in Labov's study may not likely prevail in Cameroon, irrespective of the plausibility of the model of social structure upon which the investigation is based. One can therefore predict that an investigation to determine the pattern of correlation between social status and linguistic variables in Cameroon is likely to obtain results similar to the one reported in Labov's (1966) study if the investigation is based on a model of social structure similar to the one proposed in this study and if informants are evaluated in terms of their knowledge of educated Cameroon English phonological features.

2.2 The Correlation between Gender and Linguistic Variables

Like social class, female-male linguistic differences have witnessed significant scholarly attention. An attempt would be made to critically appreciate some of the investigations that have been carried out in different communities to investigate these differences. It seems to be a universal view that men and women have distinctive speech features and, in this situation, women are said to be more likely to use stigma-free forms than men. It should be noted that sociolinguistic interest in investigating female-male linguistic differences started only in the second phase of the 20th century. Chambers (1995) reveals that most scholars who were interested in the speech of men and women before the second phase of the 20th century were mostly social psychologists, sociologists, dialectologists and anthropologists. Before assessing whether it is a truism that women are more likely to use less stigmatized linguistic features than men, as is claimed in most studies, it would be necessary to distinguish what has been referred to in the literature as "sex-based" and "gender-based" linguistic differences.

2.2.1 Sex-based and Gender-based Linguistic Variability. Most studies that seek to establish female-male linguistic differences do not always draw the significant dichotomy that exists between the terms "gender" and "sex". But Chambers (1995:103 ff) distinguishes between what he calls the "biology of masculinity and femininity" on the one hand and the "sociology of masculinity and femininity" on the other. He argues that studies which set out to reveal what is often referred to as "linguistic sex differences" run the "risk of oversimplification" because "sex... is a biological given" whereas "gender is a social acquisition" (Chambers 1995:105). He implies that the pattern established in most sociolinguistic studies about the speech of men and women does not depend on the fact that men and women are biologically different, but on the fact that they have different social roles to play. He goes further to distinguish between a grammatical gender and a social gender. A grammatical gender is expressed "by inflectional affixes on nouns and sometimes by concord or agreement inflections on part of speech in construction with nouns" (Chambers 1995:105). In grammatical gender, such grammatical categories as masculine, feminine and neuter are often distinguished (see Coates 1986). A social gender on the other hand refers to the socio-cultural differences that exist between male and female speakers (Chambers, P.105). He maintains that any failure to distinguish between gender (with a social meaning) and sex has the tendency to disguise "significant correlations of linguistic variation with gender on the one hand and with sex on the other" (Chambers ibid: 103f). His argument, in a nutshell, is that sex-based variability, which is biologically determined, is very different from gender-based variability, which is socially determined.

2.2.2 Is there a Universal Pattern of Correlation between Male and Female Speech? From many sociolinguistic studies there seems to be a universal pattern of correlation between male and female speech where it is claimed that female speakers are more likely to use more prestige or stigma-free linguistic features than their male counterparts. Such studies, conducted mostly in the Western world, that provide evidence to support the claim will be examined and the reasons explaining the claim shall equally be underscored. Besides, studies conducted out of the Western world that tend to contradict the claim shall equally be appreciated, as a prerequisite for the main argument in this book — that the correlation pattern between a social category and linguistic variables depends on the realities of the setting where the investigation is carried out.

2.2.2.1 Evidence Supporting the Claim. Many sociolinguistic studies have reported male-female linguistic differences. One of such investigations is Fischer's (1958) study. He investigated the linguistic variable (ng) in a small village near Boston in the United States of America. He submitted 24 school children into a test to find out how their pronunciation varied between /n/, the sub-standard variant and /ŋ/, the standard variant in words such as *running* and *coming*. He discovered that there was actually a significant difference between the pronunciation of female and male speakers. The standard variant /ŋ/ was far more frequent in the speech of female speakers than in the speech of   male speakers.

Trudgill (1974) submitted into a further investigation the same linguistic variable Fischer (1958) studied. This time, the variable was studied in Norwich and his findings were not different from those of Fischer. In all social classes women had less cases of the stigmatised variant /ən/ than men.

In Sydney, like Fischer and Trudgill, Horvath (1985) submitted the *ng* variable to an investigation. Her findings were slightly different from previous findings, though the general correlation pattern between linguistic variables and the sex of the speakers was not contradicted. She discovered that the linguistic variable (ng) had three variants and not only two as previously established. The variants were /ɪn/, /ɪŋ/ and /ɪŋk/. The third variant /ɪŋk/ was noticed to be common only in lexical items containing the morpheme *thing* as in *anything*, *everything*, *nothing* and *something*. The most important observation in her study is the fact that the standard variant /ɪŋ/ was more frequent in the speech of women than what was observed in the speech of men. The variant actually occurred in the speech of three female groups, but was observed only in the speech of one male group.

Linguistic differences between men and women seem to be a universal tendency. Like the cases of Boston's villages, Norwich and Sydney, Wolfram (1969) studied the speech of Black Americans in the city of Detroit. The informants were selected according to gender and social class. He considered eight phonological and eight grammatical variables in his study, but we shall limit the discussion to phonological evidence, since the scope of this work does not include the domain of grammar. In the investigation of the (th) variable among Detroit speakers of Black English vernacular (BEV) at morpheme-media and final positions, it was realised that the variable had four different variants: standard /θ/, labiodental /f/, alveolar /t/ or a complete absence of the sound which was represented by the symbol ø. In initial position, the obvious variant was the standard /θ/, but this is of little interest because almost all his subjects rightly produced the variant in initial position. At word-medial position in such words as *nothing* and at word-final position as in *tooth*, the following striking realisations were observed:

Category	nothing	tooth
/θ/	/nɔθɨŋ/	/ʉθ/ or /uθ/
/f/	/nɔtɨn/	/tuf/
/t/	/nɔfɨn/	infrequent /tut/
ø	/nɔɨθn/	(/w#ɪmi/)
(Wolfram 1969:92)		

He calculated the percentage of the non-standard variants as opposed to the standard one. Interestingly, the two gender groups in each social class had significant differences in the way they produced the non-standard variants. Fewer non-standard variants were observed in the speech of women than in the speech of their counterparts. Wolfram's (1969) next phonological investigation was focused on whether there was the absence or presence of post-vocalic /r/, an investigation somewhat similar to Labov's (1966) study. He realised that the constriction of /r/, which is often considered a prestige in rhotic accents, was more frequent among female speakers.

A sociolinguistic study which has established a pattern similar to the one discussed so far is that of Macaulay (1977). He subjected his Glasgow English speakers to a test to find out how they varied between /ɪ/, the standard Glaswegian English variant and /ʌʌ/, the stigmatised Glasgow vernacular variant. Like previous studies, he realised that women preferred the prestige variant and men's speech was characterized by the non-prestige variant.

In Belfast, like in other communities, women take the lead in approximating standard linguistic variants. Milroy and Milroy (1978) considered two social dimensions in their Belfast study: age and gender. They investigated the following linguistic variable: /ʌ/, the stigmatized Belfast vowel in such words as "pull", "took" and "look". This stigmatized variant was reported to be rampant among Belfast speakers, but the frequency was observed to be more in the speech of men. In all age groups, male speakers used it more than female ones.

The second linguistic variable investigated in the Belfast study was *th*. In Belfast, this variable is deleted inter-vocally in words such as "bother", "mother", "other", "together" such that "mother", for instance, is rendered as /mɔːər/. This deletion is reported to occur about 70% of the time in the speech of male speakers, 30% among older women and 25% among younger women.

The third linguistic variable investigated in the Belfast study by the Milroys was the variable /ɛ/. This variable has the variants: /æ/ and /ɛ/ in Belfast English. The variant /æ/is the sub-standard variant that occurs in words such as "step", "bet" and "peck", instead of the standard variant /ɛ/. The Milroys discovered that the men used the regional or the sub-standard variant almost all the time whereas the women used all the variants, but tended to use the standard variant more than the non-standard variant.

The last variable considered in the Belfast study is (a). Milroy and Milroy (1978) reported that the variants for this variable in Belfast involve the variants: /a/ and /ɛ/, but sometimes variants such as /a/, /aə/, /ɔ/ and /ɔə/ are also heard in the speech of the speakers. They noticed that men had lesser occurrence of the standard variant than women. It was equally noticed that younger women had an edge over middle-aged women in approximating the standard variant.

In all studies examined so far, there is enough evidence for the claim that men and women have different linguistic features and, in this situation, women tend to have an edge over men. But what explains this male-female linguistic speech pattern which shows that female speakers tend to have an edge over their male counters in choosing stigma-free linguistic features?

2.2.2.2 Reasons Explaining the Claim. In the above section, the claim that female speakers tend to have an edge over male speakers in choosing prestige or stigma-free linguistic features has been substantiated with different studies carried out mostly in Western societies. We shall now examine reasons that have been advanced to justify this tendency in which female speakers are said to have an edge over their male counterparts in the choice of prestige linguistic features.

Some scholars (e.g. Briscoe 1978, Gorski 1987, Kimura 1987, and Chambers 1995) have attributed physiological or biological differences between men and women to be at the origin of female-male linguistic differences. Women and men are said to have different endocrinal secretions which have different effects on their behavior (Briscoe 1978). Progesterone is said to be a female hormone and testosterone is that of their male counterparts. The presence of these hormones in the first few weeks after conception is said to determine the development of the genitalia. In the gestation period, the presence of these hormones then determines sex-appropriate behavior.

The view equally suggests that men and women have different brain structures. Given this sex-based brain differentiation, Kimura (1987:135) then hypothesised what is referred to as "sexual dimorphism in brain asymmetry" (Kumura, ibid.) which means the degree to which the left and right hemispheres of the brain are specialised for different functions. Women's brains are said to be more apt or more specialised for linguistic functions than men's. The implication here is that there is a lower incidence of aphasia in women. If there is any damaged on one part of the female brain, their language capacity is less likely to be disrupted. Sex-based brain asymmetry has therefore been considered in previous studies as an explanation for the fact that women tend to have an advantage over men in verbal abilities.

Another view holds that women use more prestige forms of speech because they are endowed with special sociolinguistic and verbal abilities. These special abilities are said to be independent of all other factors which have been advanced to be at the origin of gender differences in speech. Chambers (1992:132), for instance, confirms that WC women in Ballymacarrett have a linguistic repertoire that allows them to converse on equal linguistic terms with the sluggards from the shipyard living next door and with the tuffs from the law office across the corridor at work. They are said to have the linguistic flexibility that enables them to alter speech as warranted by the social circumstances (Chambers, ibid.).

Besides the factors underscored above which have been advanced to explain male-female linguistic differences, there is equally what has been referred to in the literature as *face*. According to Deuchar (1988:31), women tend to use more standard features of speech because of an interpersonal strategy known as *face*. The notion of *face* presents a situation whereby participants in a discourse struggle to maintain a certain degree of self-esteem. The notion presupposes that in a conversational exchange, there is an interactional tension between the desire for individual autonomy or self-reliance (i.e. *negative face*) and the desire for approval or cooperativeness (*positive face*) (Chambers 1995:131 after Brown and Levinson 1978). Chambers (ibid.) goes further to add that "Social intercourse normally requires paying attention to the other participant's face while protecting one's own". How does this then account for the fact that women use more prestige forms of speech? Deucher (P.31) explains that

> The use of standard speech, with its connotation of prestige, appears suitable for protecting the face of a relatively powerless speaker without attracting that of the addressee. (Deucher, 1988:31.)

The implication of Deucher's explanation is that the notion of *face* is more observable in situations where the participants have unequal power. Women are said to be always conscious of their weaker position and that is why they face a certain challenge in interacting with men. As a result of this social challenge, they struggle to use linguistic tools to maintain their own *face*. According to Chambers (1995), Deucher's notion of *face* is just a "little more than a sketch" and for it to serve as a reliable explanation for female-male linguistic variability, it needs to be further tested.

The notion of status-consciousness has also been suggested as a possible source of gender differences in speech. According to Trudgill (1972: 182f),

> Women in our society are more status conscious than men, generally speaking, and are therefore more aware of the social significance of linguistic values. (Trudgill, ibid.)

Two reasons are said to justify why women tend to be "more conscious of the social significance of linguistic values" (Trudgill, ibid.). The first reason, according to Trudgill (ibid: 182), is that

> The social position of women in our society is less secure than that of men, and, usually, subordinate than that of men. It may be therefore, that it is more necessary for women to secure and signal their social status linguistically and in other ways, and they may for this reason be more aware of the importance of this type of signal. (This will be particularly true of women who are not working). (Trudgill, ibid.)

Trudgill projects women in the above quotation to be a socially inferior group which uses language as a tool to compensate for their limitations. In other words, women use language to close the gap that exists between them and men.

The second reason, according to Trudgill, why women are more status-conscious is that

> Men in our society can be rated socially by their occupation, their earning power, and perhaps by their other abilities-in other words by what they *do*. For the most part, however, this is not possible for women. It may be, therefore, that they have instead to be rated on how they *appear*. Since they are not rated by their occupational success,

other signals of status, including speech, are correspondingly more important. (Trudgill, 1974:183)

The two reasons tend to suggest that women have a social disadvantage and, as a result, use language to neutralise the gap or to raise their social status to be equal to or to be above that of men. In this attempt to be status-conscious, women are influenced by the concepts of *femininity* and *masculinity* on the one hand, and the concepts of *overt* and *covert* prestige on the other (Trudgill, ibid.). When women are conscious of the concept of femininity, they feel that there is an extra pressure on them to sound more correct and refined. A woman is said to have been interviewed in a Norwegian dialect survey. When asked why she preferred the standard pronunciation of egg /ɛg/ instead of /æg/ which was observed to characterize men's speech, she replied that "/æg/ isn't *done* for a woman." The implication of the statement is that sub-standard speech may be good for men and not at all good for women. This is a testimony that, because of the concept of femininity, women tend to be pressurised to use prestige forms of speech. Men on the other hand are pressurised by the concept of masculinity not to bother about prestige or standard speech. They are said to prefer non-standard linguistic features as a signal of group identity and as an indication that they are socially different from women.

Trudgill (ibid.) also associates women's tendency to be status-conscious to their sensitivity to the concept of overt prestige. Men are said to prefer the concept of covert prestige. Each of these forms of prestige has its rewards. In the survey of Norwich urban dialect, Trudgill (ibid.) asked his informants to take part in a "self-evaluation test", in order to find out what the informants believed was the exact nature of their speech, as opposed to what Trudgill appreciated it to be. Words were read with standard and sub-standard pronunciations and the informants were asked to say which of the pronunciations was theirs. Trudgill (ibid.) analysed the result and realised that 84% of those who did not use the standard variant stated that they did not do so; 16 % of users of non-standard forms claimed to use the standard forms, when they did not, in actual fact, use them. Trudgill realised that 60 % of users of the standard variant were accurate in their report and 40% of them actually claimed to use the sub-standard pronunciation when they, in fact, used the standard variants. Such speakers who claimed to use less *statusful* variants than they actually used, Trudgill described them as *under-reporters*. The 16 % users of less *statusful* variants who claimed to use the standard variants, when they did not, were described as *over-reporters* (Trudgill, ibid.).

In the analysis of the above scores on the basis of gender, Trudgill realised that, of the 40 % under-reporters, half were men and half, women. But of the 16 % over-reporters, all were women. Over-reporting therefore introduces the concept of *overt prestige* and under-reporting introduces that of *covert prestige*. Each of these forms of prestige has its rewards. Women are therefore said to be sensitive to the concept of overt prestige because its speakers are rated as being "more intelligent, ambitious, self-confident and socially superior" (Trudgill, ibid.). Men, on the other hand, are said to prefer covert prestige because its speakers are perceived to be "serious, talkative, good-natured and amusing" (Trudgill, ibid.).

The notion of status consciousness is therefore said to be at the origin of women's use of standard forms of speech. Such a postulation sounds quite convincing, but it needs to be further investigated, especially in communities where English is not used as a mother tongue. Trudgill (ibid.) actually x-rays women as a group which is socially disadvantaged and, as a result, they tend to use language as a weapon to neutralise the gap. Explanations of this nature which under-grade women have often provoked bitter criticisms from feminist writers. Cameron (1988:5 f), for instance, argues that measuring instruments, analytical tools, theoretical assumptions, techniques of interpretation in most studies which set out to investigate linguistic differences between men and women have been full of bias and subjectivity. She insists that "this bias must not be ignored, because studies of *difference* are not just disinterested quests for truth but in an unequal society inevitably have a political dimension" (Cameron, ibid.).

Isolation from the immediate concerns of the day has equally been seen as a possible reason why men and women find themselves at two opposing poles of a linguistic continuum. Cicero in *De Orator III, XII,* quoted in Chambers (1995:124), presents a situation whereby his mouthpiece, Crassus, fails to meet up with the elegant speech of his mother-in-law. In justifying why women have an edge over men in linguistic matters, Cicero maintains that "women more easily preserve the ancient language unaltered, because, not having experience of the conservation of a multitude of people, they always retain what they originally learned". Cicero also suggests that Crassus' mother-in-law, whose speech represents the purity of women's speech, is preserving the elegant accent of her father and forefathers.

Some of Cicero's statements are questionable. How convincing is it to say that when the womenfolk are less exposed to people with different accents, they are likely to have prestige forms of speech? Language constantly evolves and sometimes new and innovative forms are more prestigious and admirable than old-fashioned forms. In effect, the act of living within a confinement does not appear to be a convincing reason for women to have prestige forms of speech. In practice, isolation may even be a setback as far as speech production is concerned. In Belfast, for instance, Chambers (1995: 126) reports that men are linguistically less proficient than women because they are said to live a circumscribed type of life.

2.2.2.3 Evidence Contradicting the Claim. In most Western societies, the view that female speakers tend to use more prestige linguistic features tends to be unambiguously established. But in non-Western societies with different sociolinguistic and cultural realities, the situation tends to be different. In Japan, for instance, Edwards (1903), quoted in Jesperson (1921: 243) and Chambers (1995:139), contrasts Japanese female-male speech pattern with what is obtained in European countries and concludes that Japanese women are more prone to stigmatized forms than their male counterparts. He explains this correlation pattern with the fact that Japanese women are not as educated as their male counterparts.

The picture painted in the Middle East equally appears to be different from the general tendency observed in Western communities. Ferguson (1956, 1959a, and 1970) reveals that most Middle East nations are characterized by a diglossic situation where there is the High and the Low varieties of the Arabic language. The *High* variety, also known as Literary Arabic, is used in all formal situations like news broadcasts, lectures and sermons. The *Low* variety is used in all informal situations. Given this diglossic situation, most studies which have investigated female–male linguistic differences in the Middle East (Schmidt 1974, Salam 1980, Bakir 1986) tend to associate men with the *High* variety and women with the *Low* variety. Such a pattern seems to reverse the pattern established in Western communities, as it suggests that men use more prestige forms than women. But Ibrahim (1986: 115) argues that Literary Arabic which is considered the High variety is not necessarily the prestige variety within the Arab world. He sees Literary Arabic as the language of those who have attended the best public schools and, as a result, its prestige is limited to very special situations. In effect, it is *Low* Arabic which is priced by Arabic speakers as the prestige variety. It is not surprising that Abd-el-Javad (1987: 3604) investigated the variable /q / in Nablus and Baghdad and the variants /g/ and /ʔ/, the sub-standard variants, were seen by his informants as the variants they were striving to produce. The standard variant /q/ was seen to be old-fashioned. One can therefore notice that the notions of *prestige* and *standard* which enjoy the same meaning in the Western world actually have different meanings in the Arabic community. Chambers (1995: 142) confirms in the following excerpt that the two notions can be used interchangeably in the Western world:

> Most people asked to evaluate speakers using standard and non-standard speech forms, will judge the standard users more favourable, attribute to them higher status and

material success, and generally associate with them the trappings of prestige. (Chambers, ibid.)

In an area like the Middle East where the notion of prestige is instead associated with the sub-standard or *Low* variety of the language, one would logically understand why men are said to have more standard forms of speech than women.

It should be noted that apart from a few statements, little or no serious research works have been carried out to investigate female-male linguistic differences in communities where the New Englishes are used. In a New English context, such as Cameroon, where speakers of a Western variety of English are ridiculed rather being admired, what is likely to be the pattern of correlation between linguistic variables and gender? What constitutes prestige and stigmatized English linguistic features in such a context, which has cultural and sociolinguistic realities different from those of the Western world?

2.3 The Correlation between Ethnicity and Linguistic Variables

Ethnicity, like the other sociolinguistic variables discussed so far, has been one of the main concerns in sociolinguistic investigations. But it should be noted from the outset that the notion of ethnicity does not enjoy the same meaning in both the Western World and Africa. In a place like the US and other Western countries, it simply refers to Black-White distinction. But in Africa, it refers to different tribal backgrounds with different linguistic substrata. This section is therefore an attempt to appreciate the correlation pattern that has been established in previous literature between this social category and linguistic variables in terms of substrate effects and not in terms of Black-White linguistic distinction. Earlier studies in New English contexts have actually concluded that this sociolinguistic variable correlates significantly with linguistic variables. But this correlation pattern is proven in later studies to have been overstated and this explains why there is need to restudy this sociolinguistic variable in Cameroon, one of the New English contexts. We shall therefore examine what existing literature postulates to be the pattern of correlation between this social category and linguistic variables.

In Nigeria, for instance, the pattern of correlation between ethnicity and linguistic variables has been discussed, for example, in Bamgbose (1971), Jibril (1982) and Awonusi (1986). The three major tribes in Nigeria, Yoruba, Igbo and Hausa, are said to have significant distinctive linguistic features. The Yoruba and Igbo accents constitute the Southern accent and this is contrasted with the Northern Hausa accent. Within the Southern accent, there are equally marked differences between Yoruba and Igbo accents. Awonusi (1986: 558), for instance, demonstrates that the vowel /ɛ/ characterises the speech of Igbo speakers of English and in Yoruba English the vowel is heard as /a/. In this case, words such as "learn", "early", "thirty" and "service" are pronounced by Igbo speakers as /lɛn, ɛli, tɛti, sɛvis/ respectively, and by Yoruba speakers as /lan, ali, tati, savis/ respectively. The word "your" is also reported to be pronounced by Igbo speakers as /jua/and this is contrasted with the Yoruba pronunciation of /ja/.

Bamgbose (1971) and Jibril (1982) also draw the demarcation line between Southern and Northern accents. The Hausa speakers are said to insert /i/ to simplify consonant clusters as in *Eng[i]lish, fruit[i]ful, B[i]ritish* and *resig[i]nations*. It is also reported that in Hausa English, the schwa /ə/ is replaced by /a/, as opposed to /ɔ/, which characterises Southern English. The consonants /θ/ and /ð/ are also realised in Hausa speech as /s/ and /z/ respectively, as opposed to /t/ and /d/ which characterize Southern English.

In Ghana as well, ethnicity is said to correlate significantly with linguistic variables. Bobda (2000a: 260), after Sey (1973:145), testifies that Cape Coast speakers of English in Ghana produce RP /ʌ/ as /ɛ/, as contrasted with mainstream Ghanaian English vowel /a/. Bobda (ibid.) also reports that speakers of the Ga tribe use /ɔ/ instead of /ɛ/, observed in the speech of Cape Coast speakers and /a/ which characterizes mainstream Ghanaian English.

Ethnic variations have also been observed in Kenya. Kanyoro (1991: 409) attests that Kalenjin speakers of English use /ʧ/ and /ʤ/, /b/and /p/, /k/ and /g/ without any distinction. In such a situation, words such as "cheer" and "jeer", "backery" and "packery", "coca" and "gogakola", "cake" and "gake" are said to be homophones. He also testifies that Luo speakers make no distinction between /ʃ/ and /s/. In this case, words such as "sugar" and "shirt" are pronounced as /suga/ and /sat/ respectively. Central Kenya Bantu speakers are also said to lack the distinction between /l/ and /r/, /ʃ/ and /ʧ/ and tend to produce the following pairs of words as homophones: *lorry/rorry, lice/rice, land/rand* (Kanyoro 1991:409 and Bobda, 2000:260), a tendency reported to be the linguistic peculiarity of some tribes in Cameroon, as shall be underscored later on in the discussion. Central Kenya Bantu speakers equally "pre-nasalize the voiced stops /b/, /d/, /g/, pronouncing *bad* as *mband, red* as *rend, lad* as *land, goat* as *ngoat"* (Bobda, ibid). It is also postulated that speakers of Western Bantu languages lack the distinction between voiced stops and fricatives and their corresponding voiceless segments. In this case, words such as "bible", "drive", "jet", "guest" are rendered "piple", "trife", "chet", "kest" respectively (Bobda, ibid.).

In Cameroon, as pointed out above, a number of statements have equally been made on the correlation between ethnicity and linguistic variables. Mushing (1989), for instance, reported that the diphthong /əʊ/ is not frequent in the speech of Banso speakers of English who have Lamnso as their mother-tongue. Lamnso is said to lack the diphthong /əu/ and, as a result, its speakers replace it with /u/. In this situation, words such as "note", "load", "soap" are pronounced /nut, lud, sup/ for RP /nəut, ləud, səup/ and for Cameroon English (CamE) "n[o]te", "l[o]d", "s[o]p" respectively.

Interestingly, Bobda (2000:3.) argues that some RP segments such as /ʌ/ and the NURSE vowel /ɜ:/, which are lacking in the speech of most African accents of English, cannot be attributed to the influence of the speakers' source languages, although these vowels (/ʌ/ and /ɜ:/) are completely absent in the vowel system of all African languages. He argues that all African languages have the same seven vowel system: /i, e, a, ɛ, ɔ, o, u/ and if the cause of the absence of RP /ʌ/ and /ɜ:/ could be attributed to the influence of the mother-tongue, then why is it that "the substitutes for non-occurring native English vowels are not the same throughout African Englishes[?]" (Bobda, ibid:3). He goes further to report that RP /ʌ/, for instance, is realised as /a/ in Ghana, /ɔ/ in Sierra Leone, Nigeria and Cameroon and also as /a/ in Kenya. He also reveals that RP /ɜ:/ is produced as /ɛ/ in Ghana and Cameroon and as /a/ in Nigeria and Kenya. He ascribes the absence of /ʌ/ and /ɜ:/ in African accents of English to the sub-standard colonial speech patterns and some intralingua factors like vowel assimilation, the influence of spelling and the processes known as "sui generis processes" (See Bobda 1994 for a detailed account of these processes). He also attributes the reason for the absence of RP /ʌ/ and /ɜ:/ to the learning context which does not have the traditional native English model as the target.

It has equally been observed that some Bafut speakers of English do not have the sounds /p/ and /r/. In this situation, they are replaced by /b/ and /l/ respectively. Words such as "Paul" and "Peter" are realised as "baul" and "beter"; and the words "ruler" and "Land Rover" are produced as "luler" and "Land Lover" respectively.

In spite of the numerous studies that have reported the significant correlation between ethnicity and linguistic variables, there is need for a further investigation in a place like Cameroon, given that in these previous studies the impact of other non-linguistic variables, such as education, has hardly been considered in investigating the correlation between this social category and linguistic variables. It has been noted through observation that educational attainment can significantly neutralize the impact of substrate effects. If this is eventually proven to be true, it implies that it can be very misleading if certain linguistic features are "stamped" on speakers of a given linguistic substratum without making reference to the level of education of such speakers.

2.4 The Correlation between Regionality and Linguistic Variables

The preoccupation of this section is to examine what has been established in existing literature to be the correlation pattern between regionality and linguistic variables. Like the other non-linguistic variables examined so far in this chapter, the region of a speaker is said to have a significant correlation with linguistic variables. Hughes and Trudgill (1979:3) point out that in the UK, for instance, phonological features are distributed significantly according to the region of the speakers. They maintain that in the North and Midlands of England, the vowel /ʌ/ is gradually being replaced by /ʊ/ and, as a result, pairs of words such as "put" and "putt", "could" and "cud" tend to be perfect homophones. In this region, words such as "mud" and "mood" are also homophonous (Hughes and Trudgill, ibid.). This situation is contrasted with what is obtained in places such as Wales, Scotland, Ireland and the South Midlands of Britain where the homophonous pairs cited above are clearly distinguished by /ʊ/ and /ʌ/ respectively.

It is also reported that in South-Eastern England, when one of these vowels [ɑː, ɔː, ɜː, ɪə, ɛə, ə] occurs before another vowel, a /r/ is automatically inserted. Hughes and Trudgill (ibid.:33) testify that this intrusive r is a prestige in South Eastern England, but the phenomenon is not observed at all in Scottish and RP accents. In Scotland and Wales, it is realised as the flap /ɾ/. Speakers from the South West of England and Ireland have the retroflex approximant /ɻ/ as its equivalent (Hughes and Trudgill, ibid.).

It is also pointed out that in most urban regional accents in England, /h/ tends to be silent. In this case, "art" and "heart", "arm" and "harm" tend to be perfect rhymes. In the accents of Newcastle, Ireland and North East of England, this tendency is not observed (Hughes and Trudgill, ibid.). In Norfolk, parts of Suffolk, Essex, Cambridgeshire, Northamptonshire, Bedfordshire, Leicestershire, Lincolnshire and Nottinghamshire as well, /j/ is dropped before /uː/ after all consonants. Words such as "pew", "beauty", "view", "few" and "music" are uttered as /puː, buːtu, vuː, fuː, muːzik/ respectively (Hughes and Trudgill, ibid.) One can guess that such a tendency is the influence of American English, given that this linguistic tendency is also observable in American English and American English is said to be penetrating all the corners of the planet earth.

The following table (taken from Hughes and Trudgill, 1979: 39) presents a summary of accent variation in the UK:

Table 2c: Accent variation according to region in the UK (Hughes and Trudgill, 1979: 39).

	/^/ in mud	/aː/ in path	/aː/ in palm	/iː/ in hazy	/r/ in bar	/uː/ in pool	/h/ in harm	/g/ in sing	/j/ in few	/ei/ in gate
Scotland and North Ireland	+	-	-	-	+	-	+	-	+	-
North East	-	-	+	+	-	+	+	-	+	-
Central North	-	-	+	-	-	+	-	+	+	-
C. Lancs	-	-	+	-	+	+	-	+	+	+
Merseyside	-	-	+	+	-	+	-	+	+	-
Humberside	-	-	+	+	-	+	-	-	+	-
N.W Midlands	-	-	+	-	-	+	-	+	+	+
E. Midlands	-	-	+	-	-	+	-	-	-	+
W. Midlands	-	-	+	+	-	+	-	+	+	+
Wales	+	-	+	+	-	+	-	-	+	-
S. Midlands	+	+	+	+	-	+	-	-	-	+
E. South-West	+	-	-	+	+	-	-	-	+	+
W South-West	+	-	-	+	+	+	-	-	+	-
South-East	+	+	+	+	-	+	-	-	+	+
East Anglia	+	+	+	+	-	+	+	-	-	+

The table is fairly self-explanatory. The positive signs indicate the presence of the segments in the different regions of the UK and the negative signs indicate the absence of these segments. As the table clearly shows, phonological features in the UK are significantly distributed according to the region of the speakers. But what is likely to be the situation in contexts where English is not used as a mother tongue? Does accent also vary according to the regions of the speakers, as is reported in the Western world? The answers to these questions are attempted in Chapter Four.

2.5 The Correlation between Age and Linguistic Variables

Does age also correlate significantly with linguistic variables, as is the case with other sociolinguistic variables? Studies that have investigated the correlation between age and linguistic variables are mostly conducted in the Western world and they tend to be unanimous in asserting that each age group has unique sociolects. Younger speakers, for instance, are said to be distancing themselves from the speech of older speakers, which is considered to be more conservative and standard.

Before examining this view in greater detail, it is worthwhile to first of all review Labov's (1964) view which tends to be contrary to the general pattern established in other communities. According to Labov (1964: 89), the acquisition of standard features of speech is a "process of acculturation" whereby adolescents tend to be linguistically similar to "the predominating pattern of the adult community" (Labov, ibid.). He, in fact, acknowledged that young people have acquired significantly "the norms of [linguistic] behavior which govern the adult community" (Labov, ibid.). Chambers (1995: 155) sees Labov's conclusion "to be partly an artefact of his method". He argues that each age group has its peculiarities and these peculiarities are marked at the physical, attitudinal and levels linguistic. Each of these levels is said to be reflective of the other. At the physical level, he reveals that childhood is marked by "superficial androgyny with boys and girls similar in height, weight, musculature and other physical characteristics" (Chambers 1995: 147). Adolescence is said to be marked by the emergence of visible sex differences, considerable gain in height without a corresponding weight gain, except in very specific cases. Early adulthood pushes the peculiarities of adolescence aside and embraces the traits of an idealised 25-year-old– wrinkle-free, clear-eyed and slim wasted (Chambers 1995: 147). He further reveals that as one advances in age, new physical features emerge– "wrinkling skin, weight re-apportionment in chest and abdomen, greying hair and, for men, receding hairlines" (Chambers 1995: 148). Old age is said to be equally marked by bald heads.

Like physical traits, attitudes and style of dressing are said to be good markers of age. In almost every society, different age groups can be distinguished from their dressing. Chambers (1995) reports that younger people are very innovative in their attires and tend to be always conscious of mode or fashion. The older generation tends to be conservative and less concerned with fashion. These different styles of dressing also reflect attitudes. The younger generation is said to be generally dynamic and flexible and this is contrasted with the conservatism of older people.

Besides physical traits, dressing and attitudes, language, certainly the most important, is also one of the means through which different age groups can be identified. According to Crystal (1987: 19), there is a clear and unmistakable relationship between age and language "since no one would have any difficulty identifying a baby, a young child, a teenager, a middle-aged person or a very old person from a tape recording" (Crystal, 1987:19). Sharing the same view, Chambers (1995:149) maintains that "A person's speech is such a reliable indicator of age that we can usually guess the age of telephone callers within seconds of hearing their voice for the first time" (Chambers 1995:149).

Pitch is one of the main indicators of age in speech (Crystal 1987 and Chambers 1995). Pitch is said to result from the rate of vibration of the vocal cords. It is measured in cycles per second or Herz (Hz). The average pitch of a person's voice is called the fundamental frequency (fo) and this fo decreases as one gets older. Chambers (1995:150), after (Helfrich 1979: 80), testifies that babies just delivered have a mean fo of about 500 Hz; infants who are already talking, around 450 Hz. By the time one reaches adulthood, the mean fo has reduced to 225 Hz and 120 Hz for women and men respectively. Chambers however remarks that pitch is rather an indicator and not a marker of age because it manifests itself in every speaker in almost the same way. By this, he implies that pitch has little social significance because it does not correlate with age in any significant way.

At this point, one would want to know which sociolects are associated with the different age groups. Chambers (1995:158) identifies three formative periods in the acquisition of age-based sociolects: periods of childhood, adolescent and young adulthood. In childhood, he says, "the vernacular develops under the influence of family and friends"; in adolescence, "vernacular norms tend to accelerate beyond the norms established by the previous generation, under the influence of dense net-working" and in young adulthood "standardisation tends to increase, at least for the sub-set of speakers involved in language-sensitive occupations" (Chambers, 1995:158). He believes that no large-scale or significant changes take place in the speech of individuals from middle age onward because their sociolects are already fixed or permanent. Each of the three formative periods will be examined in greater detail below.

2.5.1 *Childhood under Peer and Parental Influence.* Chambers (1995) establishes that, in spite of the fact that children's first linguistic models are provided by their parents, most of their speech items are determined by their relationship with peers. He reports the case of an Italian child who grows up in Australia and ends up speaking a variety of English that is quite similar to that of his Australian peers. He also refers to the case of the "children of Scots school teachers [who] sound like their parents' students of the same age and class rather than like their parents" (Chambers, P.159). It is therefore unambiguously established in Chambers (1995) that those sociolects which characterize childhood develop more through the influence of peers rather than through parental influence.

2.5.2 *Period of Adolescence.* Chambers (1995:169) sees this period as the "transition to individuation". This transition is characterized by extremism. During childhood, it is said, these adolescents were under the total control of their parents. In most cases, they are prohibited from carrying out certain responsibilities of their own, such as, driving a car, smoking, getting married without the concern of the parents and drinking alcoholic drinks (Chambers, 1995:169). The adolescents always see this control as a "suffocating authority which they must rebel against" (Chambers, 1995:171). The rebellion, Chambers reveals, always takes two forms: physical and linguistic rebellion. At the physical

level, they dye their hair (sometimes with many colors), put on nose rings, wear torn jeans and sometimes old fashion shoes. Chambers further points out that these outer markings or physical extravagance must be judged by the elders as "frivolous" or "extravagant" in order that it fulfils its social function. He also points out that if the markers become common, they switch to something different in order to exclude outsiders. In this trend, they tend to regard elders or any other person in authority as "peeps" or "pigs" (police) or "mindfuckers" (manipulators). Peers who are non-conformists are seen as "dweeb", "dork", "nerd", "geek", "lame", "jerk" and "nimrod" (Chambers, P.171).

This rebellion is also manifested at the linguistic level. They often use specialised vocabulary or slangs. Chambers identifies a long list of these slangs which are consciously ignored in this review because the scope of the work is limited to phonology.

Popular music is said to be one of the preoccupations of adolescents. Chambers remarks that "one of the social functions of teenage music is to envelop listeners in sound and shut out the hostile adult world, as seen most obviously in "thumpers", cars with sound systems turned up so loud that the bass reverberates through the traffic noise, and in "headbangers", portable sound systems with headphones that cannot quite contain the volume being pumped into the listeners' ears" (Chambers, 1995:171-2).

What is of paramount interest in adolescents' conscious deviation from adult norms is the emergence of linguistic peculiarities which are unique to them. The choice of specific linguistic variants is primarily intended to signal the existence of their own world which is independent of the adult's world. Their success in creating such linguistic variants, Chambers (1995:172) maintains, is because "they are exposed to a wider circle of acquaintances". Having left the "suffocating" parents' confinement, they find themselves in a "free land" and 'free' here involves doing whatever thing they like.

Eckert (1988: 189) presents the social and linguistic picture of Detroit High School adolescents. Two main social groups were identified in Eckert's investigation: the Jocks and the Burnouts. The Jocks focus their lives on all school activities whereas the Burnouts reject the school premises and rather focus their activities at the outskirts of the school campus. The Jocks take part in school activities such as sports, social events and journalism. The Burnouts are used to driving old cars or pickup trucks, playing high volume music and wearing nose-rings. They are associated with drugs. They are very similar to the group of adolescents Chambers (1995) identifies and describes as social rebels.

In Detroit High School, these groups are said to constitute two contrasting poles and students often identify themselves with any of the two groups (Eckert, 1988:189). Those who belong to none of the groups see themselves as "In-betweens". The distinction between the Jocks and the Burnouts has a social class orientation. The Jocks are essentially from the MC and the Burnouts belong to the WC. The isolation of the Burnouts from the main school activities is seen as an inferiority complex accounted for by their social class. The Jocks who come from the MC, a higher social class, tend to dominate all school activities (Eckert, 1988:189).

After completing high school education, the Jocks often move on to the universities and later assume greater responsibilities. The Burnouts are said to embark on part-time jobs after school. They tend to interact mostly with old people and often involve themselves with adult recreational activities such as smoking, drinking, dating and sex.

It is interesting to note that this social picture of the groups is linguistically significant (Eckert 1988 and Chambers 1995). Eckert (1988: 200ff) studied the way the different adolescent groups in Detroit High School varied in the pronunciation of the underlined segments of words, such as, "supper", "mother", "butter" and "lumber". The variation in Detroit and other American cities like Buffalo and Chicago is said to range from the standard /ʌ/ to stigmatized /ɔ/ and /ʊ/. Eckert analyzed the speech of the three social groups of Detroit High School and discovered significant phonological variations. The Burnouts were prone to the stigmatized variants /ɔ/ and /ʊ/ and the Jocks were associated with the conservative standard /ʌ/. The "In-betweens" were actually observed to be in between as their name suggests. They used lesser of the innovative and stigmatized forms than the Burnouts and lesser of the conservative forms than the Jocks.

According to Eckert (1988: 206), these linguistic differences stem from the speakers commitment to the region. The Burnouts, for instance, use more innovative forms because these forms are associated with the urban centre and they wish to be identified with urban life. The Jocks, on the other, land do not wish to be associated with any particular region since they would probably be moving to different places for post-secondary education. As a consequence, they have lesser urban forms of speech. What is most important in Eckert's findings is the fact that adolescent groups, irrespective of the group network they belong to, have linguistic characteristics that are significantly different from what is observed in different communities to be the adult speech patterns.

Habick (1991) describes a situation very similar to the one painted by Eckert. He also identified two contrasting groups in Farmer City High School: the Burnouts and the Rednecks. Those who belonged to neither of the groups were known as *Scruffies* or outsiders. The Burnouts, like those in Detroit High School, were adolescents with a burning love for alcohol, drugs and loud music. The Rednecks, as they were referred to by the Burnouts, were those who were committed to all school activities and were usually passive to some of the extremities of the Burnouts. His investigation involved the extent to which the vowel in such words as *chew, glue, food, shoot* and *hoot* is fronted in Farmer City. He realized that the fronted /ʉ/, instead of the standard /uː/, occurred in the speech of all the subjects of the sample, irrespective of age and group network. But the degree to which this fronting occurred varied significantly. Older people (parents and grand parents) were observed to have the least frequency of the fronted variants. Among younger speakers, fronting was more observed in the speech of Burnouts than in the speech of Rednecks. In spite of the difference between the scores of the two adolescent groups, the fronting realized in the speech of the two groups significantly contrasts with that of older people.

It should be noted that the period of adulthood, which adolescent groups strive to distinguish themselves from, is actually an inescapable stage in their life. After the period of adolescence, the next stage is that of young adulthood. This is a period which has peculiarities quite different from those of other periods.

2.5.3 Adulthood under the Influence of the Concept of *Marché Linguistique*.

The adult world is significantly different from the adolescent world. Chambers (1995: 177) points out that adulthood is the period one fully assumes the responsibility of his or her own life. The choosing of a career, marriage and the setting-up of a family are usually the touchstones of this period (Chambers, 1995:177). Linguistic adjustments constitute one of the areas through which young adults project their adulthood. Sankoff and Sankoff (1973) attribute this linguistic adjustment to the concept of *Marché linguistique* which has been translated in different ways by different authors. The most appropriate translation is proposed by Chambers (P.178) as "marketplace dialect".

The concept operates on the view that some people have more (market) pressures to use standard forms of speech than others. Sankoff et al. (1989) establish that "professionals of language" (e.g. secretaries, announcers and actors) are expected by society to use more prestige forms of speech because their preoccupations involve linguistic intercourse. People like laboratory technicians, mechanics and computer programmers are said to have little or no market pressure because they have little or nothing to do with speech.

How then does the concept of "Marché linguistique" influence young adults to make linguistic adjustments? Young adults necessarily need to adjust their linguistic behaviour in order to draw a demarcation line between their new world (world of adulthood) and their former world (world of adolescence). Their adolescent life was characterised by 'extravagant' and 'rebellious' linguistic features and the market pressure requires them now to be more refined and "orderly" in their linguistic behaviour. Once they succeed in acquiring new sociolects, these features are likely to remain relatively stable till old age

(Chambers, 1995: 184). He sees this linguistic stability as a "linguistic reflex of the conservatism that often accompanies ageing" and also as "a function of the slowing of the language-learning capability beyond the critical period" (Chambers 1995: 184).

He therefore unambiguously demonstrates that the three formative periods (childhood, adolescence and young adulthood) in the acquisition of age-based sociolects correlate significantly with linguistic variables. For instance, childhood is said to be characterized by linguistic features acquired through the influence of parents and peers. Adolescence is marked by extravagant and innovative linguistic peculiarities. The period of young adulthood is a stage where the extravagance of adolescent life is replaced by refined, stable and standard linguistic forms, through the influence of market pressure. It would be interesting to assess Chambers' three formative periods through age-based studies conducted in different communities. Such an assessment will reveal whether the linguistic behaviour of the younger generation actually differs significantly from that of the older generation.

2.5.4 An Evaluation of Chambers' Three Formative Periods in the Acquisition of Sociolects.

Crystal's (1987: 19) statements seem to contradict the pattern established by Chambers in his three formative periods in the acquisition of sociolects. According to Crystal, as a speaker gets older, there is a reduction in the efficiency of his or her speech organs and as a consequence, the quality of his or her speech is bound to reduce. He argues that "The muscles of the chest weaken, the lungs become less elastic, the ribs less mobile" (Crystal, 1987:19). He adds that respiratory efficiency at age 75 is only about half at age 30 and the natural consequence is that older people "lack the ability to speak loudly, rhythmically and with good tone" (Crystal, 1987:19) He further maintains that

> The cartilages, joints, muscles, and tissues of the larynx also deteriorate, especially in men; and this affects the range and quality of voice produced by the vocal folds, which is often rougher, breathier and characterised by tremor. In addition, speech is affected by poorer movement of the soft palate and changes in the facial skeleton, especially around the mouth and jaw. (Crystal, 1987)

Crystal's postulation sounds quite interesting, but it does not, in actual fact, contradict Chambers' pattern. Crystal tends to be focusing his observation on the physiology or biology of an individual. If his postulation is actually based on the physiology of an individual, then he is very right to conclude that old speakers lack phonological ability. But Chambers, on the other hand, in concluding that older speakers use more standard forms of speech, bases his view on the sociolinguistic nature of individuals. In other words, Chambers approaches the issue from a social point of view. He sees the younger generation to be socially and linguistically more extravagant than the older generation. This implies that the two views are not in any way contradictory, given that they are approaching the issue from different perspectives. It should be noted that studies carried out in different communities give credibility to Chambers' (1995) three formative periods in the acquisition of age-based sociolects, as shall be seen in the subsequent sections.

2.5.4.1 Age-Based Sociolects in Glasgow.
An investigation carried out by Macaulay (1977: 47) reveals that there are age-graded sociolects in Glasgow. Macaulay's (ibid.) sample constituted three age groups: 10-year-olds, 15-year-olds and adults. The three age groups were categorized under three occupational groups: managers, clerks and traders. The investigation involved the use of the glottal stop /ʔ/ as the variant of /t/. The glottal stop is considered as the most striking phonological variant in Scotland and Northern England. It is reported that both teachers and government officials even make conscious efforts to dissuade students from using this stigmatized form which is considered as a "shibboleth of British WC speech" (Chambers' 1995: 190). In the evaluation of the use of the variant, Macaulay realised that its occurrence was graded according to the age and the social class of the speakers. In all social groups, the highest frequency of the stigmatized variant was registered with 10-year-olds and the lowest frequency with adults. The frequency of the stigmatized variant for 15-year-olds was observed to be in between that of adults and 10-year-olds. The pattern which emerges in this study strikingly reflects the one established in Chambers' three formative periods in which the speech of the younger generation is distant from the standard variants whereas that of the older generation is closer. It was equally discovered in the investigation that the variant was further graded according to market pressures. Clerks who have a higher tendency to use language than traders were more influenced by market pressures to minimise the use of the stigmatized glottal stop.

2.5.4.2 Age-Based Sociolects in Texas.
In order to further evaluate Chambers' three formative periods in the acquisition of age-based sociolects, we shall review what Bailey (1993) has earlier observed to be the situation in Texas. The linguistic situation in Texas is such that no distinction is often made between long and short segments. In this situation, /ɒ/ and /ɔː/ are merged to /ɑ/ as in *lost* and *walk*. There is equally a tendency for /iː/ to be reduced to /ɪ/ as in *field*, /uː/ to be reduced to /u/ as in *school* and /j/ to be deleted after /t/ followed by /u/ as in *Tuesday* (Bailey, 1993: 308).

He considered four age groups in the study: 18-29; 30-44; 45-61 and 62-95. The investigation shows that the pronunciation of the stigmatized variants was significantly graded according to age groups. Speakers between the ages of 18 and 29 tended to have the highest frequency of the stigmatized features, and as one ascends the age scale, the rate of producing the innovative features reduces systematically. This pattern goes further to give credibility to Chambers' schema. The younger generation is, in fact, more distant from standard forms of speech than the older generation.

2.5.4.3 Age-Based Sociolects in Southern Ontario.

The last study to be considered in the evaluation of Chambers' (1995) three formative periods in the acquisition of age-based sociolects is an investigation conducted in Southern Ontario reported by Chambers himself. Chambers (1995: 188f), in fact, reports an investigation he conducted in 1979 which goes further to substantiate the hypothesis that younger speakers are linguistically innovative whereas older speakers tend to be conservative. He reveals that in Southern Ontario, the southernmost and most populous part of Canada which shares a boundary with the United States on three sides, there is a significant variation in the way the last letter of the alphabet, z, is articulated. Chambers emphasises that z is produced as "zed" in almost every English-speaking community and in most languages like French and German, except in the United States where it is uttered as "zee". This pronunciation is considered stigmatized in this Canadian region known as Southern Ontario. It is said that there is even a conscious resistance to this pronunciation as a way to maintain the Canadian autonomy and to avoid American influence.

In spite of this conscious effort to avoid "zee" which is seen as an 'American shibboleth', the younger generation continues to have a high proportion of it in their speech. In the investigation conducted in 1979, Chambers (1995: 188-9) demonstrates that two-thirds of the 12-year-olds completed their recitation with "zee" as opposed to only 8% of the adult speakers. The same sample was submitted to another study 12 years after. It was discovered that the use of "zee" significantly reduces as the speakers get older. This is a clear indication that the use of standard or innovative forms of speech depends much on the age of a speaker. It should be noted that Chambers' attempt to study the speech of the same informants after a certain length of time introduces the notion of a "real time" study. He defines it as a kind of study "whereby linguists make a series of observations of similar population over many years". He contrasts a 'real time' study with an "apparent time" study. He maintains that an 'apparent time' study is "When different age groups are observed simultaneously and the observations are observed as temporal" (Chambers, 1995).

2.6 The Correlation between the Social Context and Language

Like age and the other sociolinguistic variables examined so far, the social context is said to have a significant correlation with language. We shall start the discussion in this section with the following pertinent question: Is it logical for pragmatists to have different linguistic expectations from those of purists? Those who may provide a no-answer to the question are certainly proponents of prescriptivism. Crystal establishes that prescriptivism "aims to preserve imagined standards by insisting on Norms of USAGE and criticising departures from these norms" (Crystal, 1997: 305). Prescriptivists or purists, as one may also refer to them, advocate correctness and insist that linguistic standards are non-negotiable (see, for instance, Quirk 1972 and Honey 1997).

But prescriptivism is rather unpopular among linguists who recognise the dynamic nature of language. Pragmatists actually believe that language should be seen in terms of whether it is appropriate to the social context in which it is used, and not in terms of whether it is standard or sub-standard. Hughes and Trudgill (1979), for instance, argue that the expectations of a phonologist, for instance, need not be the same as those of a pragmatist. They argue that what a phonologist may consider as standard speech may be seen by a pragmatist as inappropriate if it does not correlate with the right context. They further argue that the speech of a speaker declaring his love to a girl should logically be different from the speech used to deliver a gospel. This implies that every context has its language.

Crystal tends to share Hughes and Trudgill's (1979) view when he remarks that people have often developed the tendency to think that

> Anything which smacks of informality [should be] rigorously avoided, or if included [should be] castigated as *slang* and labelled "bad"... (Crystal, 1985:9ff)

According to him, language should be analyzed in terms of appropriateness. He argues that

> We do not, after all, use the same kind of formal language when at home or writing a letter to friends as we do when we are giving a speech or applying in writing for a job. (Crystal, ibid.)

He further reveals that language has many levels of formality and the nature of language in each level of formality is necessarily supposed to be different. He accepts that the rule of grammar, for instance, necessitates the use of, say, "whom", instead of "who", in the sentence:

> The man _____ I saw was tall and dark.

But he thinks that such rules "only distort the reality of English". He holds that it should not be the question of "whom" being correct and "who" being wrong. To him, "each is correct in certain circumstances and incorrect in others" (Crystal, ibid.).

He also rejects such rigid statements as "Never end a sentence with a preposition". He therefore concludes that the dynamism of the English language makes it difficult for one to talk of "absolute standards", given that the English language is not "a single homogeneous thing" (Crystal, ibid.). He holds that it is rather a "conglomeration of regional and social dialects, or sub-languages, all different from each other in various degrees" (Crystal, ibid: 11).

Bobda and Mbangwana (1993: 183), after Honey (1989: 137), also confirm that "top politicians like Margaret Thatcher have been shown in certain occasions to change deliberately from a posh RP accent to a more sloven accent which they know will win more confidence in a given audience". This is a further indication that standard speech, irrespective of its high prestige, may be very inappropriate in certain contexts. It should be noted that choosing between standard and sub-standard speech is similar to the choice between "overt" and "covert" prestige earlier underscored.

A speaker's sensitivity to the expectations of a context is, in fact, very crucial. A number of sociolinguists have even evaluated their samples in terms of their ability to vary their speech in different phonological styles and these phonological styles fairly correspond to different social contexts. Labov (1966), for instance, identified five phonological styles which include, in ascending order of formality, Casual Style (CS), Reading Passage Style (RPS), Word List Style (WLS), Formal Style (FS) and Minimal Pairs (MP). In his investigation, he realised that the phonological style under which speech is produced was equally instrumental in determining the choice of linguistic variants. The use of the prestige /r/, earlier discussed, was observed to be most frequent in MP, the style considered to be most formal; and least frequent in CS, except the UMC which used the prestige variant in CS with some degree of consistency.

As illustrated above, each context is said to have its own expectations and a wrong perception of context leads to inappropriateness in speech. This implies that standard speech is inappropriate in a casual context, as well as sub-standard speech will fail to have any prestige in formal contexts. It should equally be noted that in certain situations, especially in communities different from Western societies, the context imposes a completely different language and not just a variety of a given language. Schmied (1991: 180) testifies that in certain communities "If somebody uses, [for instance], English in unacceptable contexts, sanctions may even be imposed on the offender" (Schmied, ibid.). He refers to Scotton (1978: 79) who observes that

At a beer party near my home, two boys broke into talk in English. The reaction from the old men was and they said 'Who are those speaking? Are they backbiting us? They are proud. Push them out!' Although the boys had not been addressing the beer party as such but had been talking only to each other, this issue of English was regarded as an insult. (Scotton, ibid. quoted in Schmied, 1991:180)

Scotton's observation quoted above depicts a situation in Africa when people's attitude towards English was still very aggressive. It is the period people used to perceive English as a foreign asset which had to be used only by special people in special situations. But such an aggressive attitude towards English in Africa has given way to a completely new line of thinking, a line of thinking which accepts the full use of English, but dictates the variety of English to be used.

2.7 Unexplored Dimensions and Contributions

In spite of the numerous interesting and illuminating studies carried out in the Western world to investigate the correlation between the extra-linguistic variables under study and linguistic variables, the present investigation is still unique and different in many aspects. As a general statement, I maintain that, unlike most previous studies which study the correlation between social categories and linguistic variables in the Western world, this study is concerned with the correlation patterns that are likely to emerge in a New English context, such as Cameroon, a new ecological setting that has linguistic and social realities that are different from those of the Western world. Besides this general contribution, there is a specific contribution to be made as far as each of the non-linguistic variables is concerned.

As concerns gender, if we consider the general view that women use more prestige forms of speech than men, it would be interesting to know what the situation is likely to be in a community where there is no unanimity on what constitutes the prestige English accent, given that speakers of British English (the variety of English targeted in the ELT industry in Cameroon) are ridiculed rather than being admired. The implication of this situation is that the concept of prestige is fluid within the Cameroonian society and, as a result, female speakers may find themselves in ambivalent situations when it comes to choosing prestige linguistic features, whatever those prestige linguistic features are.

Another contribution this study intends to make is the fact that a speaker's occupation is investigated in terms of 'market pressure'. It would be an interesting contribution to evaluate Cameroonian speakers of English in terms of whether they show any sensitivity to the pressure put on them by their profession.

Age, like the other sociolinguistic variables considered in this study, has been given much scholarly attention, as previously underscored, but its investigation is still imperative in this study, given that findings on the correlation pattern between this sociolinguistic variable and linguistic variables tend not to be uniform in different studies. This suggests that there is a need for a study of this nature to investigate the situation in a community which is significantly different from the ones considered in previous investigations.

Numerous studies have equally been carried out to establish the correlation between ethnicity and linguistic variables, as earlier pointed out. In the situation of Cameroon, it has been observed that certain linguistic features which have been associated with Bafut and Banso speakers of English may turn out to be lacking in the speech of those who have attained a university level of education. This study therefore intends to restudy the speech of speakers from the above-mentioned tribes, who are assumed to have neutralised mother-tongue effects through education.

Regional variation in speech has also received much scholarly interest. In most of the studies, the principal objective is to establish the dialect geography of different regions. But this study has a goal that is different from those of previous studies. The study aims at investigating the degree of phonological diversity in rural and urban speech. It is observed that there is likely to be more diversity in the speech of urban speakers because they are more exposed to speakers with different linguistic backgrounds. Rural speakers on the other hand live a circumscribed type of life where there is little exposure to speakers with different accents. There is no assumption, here, that any of the groups of speakers is likely to approximate the Standard British English more than the other. Studying rural and urban speech from this perspective is certainly a positive contribution to the study of CamE speech in particular and to sociolinguistic investigation in general.

The evaluation of speakers according to the different phonological styles is also one of the contributions expected to be made in this study. Each of the phonological styles corresponds to different levels of formality. It should noted that most studies on CamE have seldom included this dimension of studying speech in the scope of their investigations.

One of the major contributions of this investigation is the study of Cameroon English speech in terms of how a speaker's mood (or the state of his or her feelings) is likely to determine his/her choice of linguistic variants. The notion of mood, in fact, enjoys more than one meaning, but we shall rather rely on the definition provided in Longman's (1987: 676) *Dictionary of Contemporary English* which defines it simply as the "state of the feelings at a particular time". I therefore rely on this definition to claim that, in addition to earlier sociolinguistic categories (gender, age, ethnicity and so on), the mood of a speaker or his or her state of the feeling at a particular time is very much likely to determine significant linguistic variability. It is worthwhile to point out that such a claim has not been made in many previous sociolinguistic studies. Clark and Clark (1977: 515) only hint, without any further details, that

> Language ... serves and is moulded by other systems in the human mind. Because it is used for converging ideas, its structure and function must reflect these ideas. (Clark and Clark, 1977:15)

In the above quotation, one important fact stands out very clearly. Language, they maintain, is 'moulded' or determined by the 'systems' in the human mind. The different moods in which a speaker finds himself or herself certainly form part of the 'systems' they imply in their statement and these moods or 'systems' should be reflected, they maintain, in the 'structure' and 'function' of language.

One would certainly like to know, at this point, the different moods or state of the feelings assumed in this dimension of the study. From a keen observation, a speaker can either be in a mood of joy, anger or fear. A speaker in a state of joy or excitement is in a positive mood, and being in such a mood, he or she is hypothesized to be psychologically prepared to be speech conscious. On the other hand, a speaker in a state of anger or fear is actually in a negative mood. In such a mood, the speaker is likely to lack the psychological preparedness to be speech conscious. This hypothesis would be examined in greater detail in Chapter Four, through the analysis and discussion of the data collected in the field.

The last contribution to be made in this study is the fact that CamE is not studied principally terms of how it deviates from native Englishes, as is the case with most previous studies on this variety of English (see, for instance, Masanga 1983, Bobda 1986, 1994, Mbangwana 1987 and Kouega 1991). Stating that the preoccupation of most previous studies on this variety of English has been to reveal deviations is not intended to devalue the invaluable contributions made in these works by the researchers. Before the early 1980s, Cameroon English had witnessed very little scholarly attention, apart from a few sociolinguistic statements made on levels other than phonology. This is an indication that studying CamE phonology at the time of Masanga (1983), and shortly after, to reveal deviations was highly innovative. It should equally be remarked that some of these previous works on CamE have made other insightful contributions, besides just revealing how the variety of English deviates from mother tongue Englishes. Bobda (1994), for instance, used the deviations inherent in CamE to establish, through the concept of trilateral process, that CamE phonology has reached a reasonable degree of predictability and definability. The present investigation, unlike previous studies on CamE, therefore, studies this variety of English from a different perspective. This involves correlating sociolinguistic and other non-linguistic variables with SBE (the variety of English promoted in the ELT industry in Cameroon) phonological variables in a new context that is culturally and sociolinguistically different from most Western societies.

Chapter Three
Method-Related Issues

3. Introduction

This chapter is devoted principally to method-related issues. The issues include a description of the informants, a presentation of the instruments for data collection, a description of the method for data collection and a description of the method for data analysis.

3.1 The Informants

The total number of informants for this study was 658. The inclusion of these informants into the sample depended on such sociolinguistic factors as level of education, sex, ethnicity, age, occupation and regionality. It is only in the investigation of the influence of the speaker's mood that the above sociolinguistic factors were not the bases for the selection of the informants. Before describing the number of informants which was evaluated for each of the social categories under study, it should be noted that there was actually an overlap in the consideration of the informants. This means that informants whose speech was analysed under, say, level of education, were still considered good candidates for another sociolinguistic variable, provided they neatly belonged to the categories of that sociolinguistic variable.

It appears necessary to provide a detailed description of the informants for each of the non-linguistic variables under study (level of education, sex, ethnicity, age, occupation, regionality, stylistic context and mood). As concerns level of education, the informants were randomly chosen from some secondary schools and universities in Cameroon. There were a total of 300 informants, evenly distributed according to the three levels of education considered in the investigation (secondary school students, undergraduate students and postgraduate students). The secondary school students were either in the first or in the second cycle of secondary school. The university students were either undergraduate or postgraduate students. The undergraduate students were either doing their first, second or third year in the university. The postgraduate students, on the other hand, were either in professional schools which have stable departments of English (e.g. Advanced Teachers' Training College Yaounde), were engaged in a Master's Degree or were carrying out research for a doctoral degree at the department of English of their respective universities (University of Yaounde 1, University of Buea and the University of Dschang).

As concerns gender, the total number of informants considered was 302, 50% of which were female speakers and the other 50% were male speakers. All the 302 informants were undergraduate university students, studying at the departments of English in their respective universities. Some of these informants constituted part of the sample for such sociolinguistic variables as level of education, age, ethnicity and regionality. The consideration of only speakers with an undergraduate university education for gender-based correlation was a conscious attempt to ensure that the correlation pattern that would emerge should not be the influence of a discrepancy in level of education.

Informants were equally evaluated according to their ethnic group. The 300 informants considered for this sociolinguistic category were chosen from such tribes as Bafut, Banso, Bangwa, Bamileke and Bakweri. Since Bafut and Banso tribes have earlier been said to display certain linguistic peculiarities, the choice of these tribes was an attempt to investigate the extent to which "mother-tongue effects" can be neutralised by educational attainment. This explains why all the informants for this social variable were either receiving university education or had completed their university studies. It should be noted that, in previous studies (e.g. Mushing 1989), it has been established that the sounds [r] and [ɔʊ] are relatively infrequent in the speech of Bafut and Banso speakers of English respectively. The inclusion of tribes such as Bamileke, Bangwa and Bakweri in the scope of the investigation was intended to provide the basis upon which comparisons and contrasts could be made in the attempt to re-assess previous statements made on the tribes of Bafut and Banso. The number of informants considered for each tribe was 60.

Concerning occupation as one of the sociolinguistic variables investigated, informants were randomly selected from three occupational groups: secondary school teachers, medical doctors and journalists. Secondary school teachers were further categorized into teachers of English and teachers of other disciplines. The choice of teachers of English and journalists was influenced by the fact they have more "market pressure" to use standard forms of speech than their counterparts in the other professions. This is because they are likely to be considered technicians of language and professionals of language respectively. Medical doctors and teachers of other disciplines, who have relatively little to do with language, were included in the sample simply as an attempt to compare and contrast their English linguistic ability with that of those who are claimed to be technicians and professionals of language. The number of informants per each occupational group (secondary school teachers of English, medical doctors, teachers of other disciplines and journalists) was 15. This relatively low number of informants can be explained by the fact that access to English-speaking medical doctors was quite difficult. The fact that only 15 medical doctors were actually submitted to a test made the investigator to consider just the first 15 speakers who served as informants for the other occupational groups. This was an attempt to have the same number of informants for all the occupational groups considered for the investigation. The relatively low number of informants for this sociolinguistic variable was, however, considered sufficient and reliable for the evaluation of speakers according to market pressures.

As concerns age, a total of 200 informants were considered for the investigation. The 200 informants, some of whom constituted part of the samples for the other sociolinguistic variables like level of education, regionality and ethnicity, were categorised into four different age groups:

. speakers between the ages of 12 and 19;
. speakers between the ages of 20 and 30;
. speakers between the ages of 31 and 49 and
. speakers above 49 years.

Each age group was made up of 50 informants. The categorization of informants into the first three age groups stated above (i.e. speakers between 12 and 19; 20 and 30; and 31 and 49 years) is similar to Chambers' (1995) second and third formative periods in the acquisition of sociolects. This implies that speakers between the ages of 12 and 19 would correspond to Chambers' adolescent group (second formative period). Those between 20 and 30 years and those between 31 and 49 years are similar to Chambers' young adults and full adult groups respectively (third formative period). His first formative period did not have any influence in the selection of informants for this study because it rather involves the period of childhood (i.e. the ages ranging from, say, one to about ten) which was not included in the scope of this investigation. The last age group stated above (i.e. speakers above the age of 49) is an additional age group considered in this study and it does not neatly equate the old age period investigated in Crystal (1987).

Informants were equally selected according to whether they were permanently based in an urban area or in a rural area. There were a total of 200 informants. Out of this number, 100 were living in rural areas and the other 100 were based in urban centres. The rural areas considered in the investigation were the following villages: Bokova, Bokwango, Nwametaw and Lewoh. These villages were chosen simply because of their feasibility to the investigator. Yaounde and Bafoussam were chosen as the urban areas for the investigation. Informants who lived in rural areas were hypothesized to have less diversity in their speech than those in the urban centres.

As concerns the evaluation of the informants according to their sensitivity to the phonological styles, the 300 speakers considered for level of education were also evaluated in different phonological styles, which fairly correspond to different levels of formality.

Informants were also chosen to assess the impact of a speaker's mood or the state of his or her feelings on speech. The attempt to choose informants to evaluate the impact of a speaker's mood on his or her speech tended to be one of the most challenging tasks. There was a strong and non-negotiable need to have the speech of the same informants recorded in the moods of anger, fear and joy. When the idea to study CamE speech according to the moods of a speaker was first conceived, there was the wish to select the required number of informants needed for the investigation and to monitor and record their speech whenever they were to find themselves in the different moods. In addition, the recording process was to take place without their knowledge. This goal was later on judged to lack feasibility. The first reason is that it could have taken too many years to have the same informants in the moods of anger, fear and joy. The second reason is that it could be quite possible to have events where the experimental subjects would be in a mood of joy, but it was very uncertain when precisely other events would come up for the same informants studied in, say, the mood of joy to be studied again in the moods of anger and fear.

Given the complexity of choosing informants to be monitored in the course of time, a new approach was conceived. The investigator, being a teacher by profession, thought of making good use of the classroom situation. A total of 16 students were tactfully singled out in the 4th year Bilingual Series class at the Advanced Teachers' Training College (Ecole Normale Supérieure) Yaounde. The number of informants who actually served as informants for this dimension of the study was finally reduced from 16 to13, and then to 11, because of reasons to be underscored in §3.3, which focuses on the method of data collection.

3.2 Instruments for Data Collection

A questionnaire was conceived to collect background information from the informants (see Appendix 1a). After the collection of background information, the informants were involved in the reading of pre-prepared sets of linguistic items containing some targeted phonological features (see Appendix 1b). The first set contained 7 pairs of linguistic items in Minimal Pairs. The second set contained 88 isolated words and each of the words involved some targeted phonological variables. The phonological variables were either segmental features or lexical stress. The third set of items displayed a series of sentences, through which the stress pattern of certain linguistic items and some segmental variables were evaluated. The last set of linguistic items was contained in a passage and the items were aimed at evaluating the informants' knowledge of lexical stress in Sentence Reading Style. It should be noted that the linguistic items on which the informants were evaluated were collected from two sources. The first source was through a keen observation of the speech of Cameroonian speakers of English. The findings from the works of previous researchers on Cameroon English (e.g. Bobda 1994 and Ngefac 1997) provided the second source.

In order to evaluate the informants in the different moods, they were involved in a transcription exercise involving certain lexical items (see Appendix 8a for the list of the lexical items). The steps involved in the evaluation of informants in different moods are described in §3.3.

3.3 Method of Data Collection

A number of strategies were used to collect data from informants, selected according to the sociolinguistic categories under study. The linguistic items were presented to the informants, selected according to the sociolinguistic variables under study, to be read aloud and their articulation was recorded with the help of a tape-recorder. It should be pointed out that, in the process of recording the informants' speech, the investigator was not at all concerned with the problem of observer's paradox, which is underscored in §2.1.1 to be fundamental in a sociolinguistic investigation. It is only during the collection of data in Casual Style and during the evaluation of informants in different moods that the investigator was sensitive to this fundamental sociolinguistic problem. This is because the informants needed to know that their speech was being recorded so that they could strive to set their speech consciousness nerves at work. But to collect data in the Casual Style and in the different moods, as shall be seen later, one needed to overcome the problem of observer's paradox, given that there was the need for free-flowing and natural speech.

In order to collect data in the different phonological styles, the speech of the informants needed to be recorded both in styles that express levels of formality (e.g. Minimal Pairs (MP), World List Style (WLS), Sentence Reading Style (SRS) and Passage Reading Style (PRS)) and in a style that expresses informality (Casual Style (CS)). The collection of data in phonological styles that express formality was not as challenging as was the case in CS. In the collection of data in styles that express formality, the informants were simply submitted to the reading of texts containing those phonological features that have been observed and re-echoed in previous studies on CamE to be problematic to Cameroonian speakers of English. As the informants read the texts aloud, a tape-recorder was used to record their articulation. It should be noted again that the informants needed to know that their speech was being tape-recorded, since they were reading in phonological styles that express formality and the formal context expects speakers to be as speech conscious as possible.

But the collection of data in the CS was altogether a different experience. This was one of the moments the investigator needed to be very sensitive to the problem of observer's paradox. The informants' speech was to be recorded in a casual context, yet they were not expected to know that their speech was being recorded. To achieve this goal, the investigator used a number of strategies. When the informants had completed the reading of texts in phonological styles that express formality, the investigator expressed gratitude to them for having allowed their speech to be tape-recorded. At this point, the investigator made gestures that gave the informants the impression that the tape-recorder was turned off. The gestures were accompanied by the fact that the tape-recorder was put away in the investigator's handbag. This further convinced them that the recording process was over. But, in actual fact, the recorder was still on. The informants were then asked to narrate an event or an incident in their lives which made them excited and another one which made them sad. The informants were expected to use less than five minutes to narrate the event or incident. They were made to understand that the focus had shifted from phonology to grammar and the exercise was to find out to what extent they could effectively express the past tense. The investigator convinced them that the aim of the exercise was simply to establish a hypothesis for another investigation to be carried out at the grammatical level, after the phonological study he was currently carrying out. Since the informants were convinced that the focus was no more on phonology and that the "grammatical exercise" was simply to establish a hypothesis, they tended to be very relaxed and as one would expect, they produced free-flowing speech.

The informants were expected to use three lexical items: "success", "happy" and "sad", the three lexical items chosen to evaluate the informants' speech in the CS. The choice of the three words was justified by two reasons. The first reason was that the informants could not avoid the words in their attempt to talk about events or incidents in their lives that had either made them excited or sad. Expectedly, they talked about their "success" in a particular exam or their "success" to be admitted into a particular school and so on, which made them to be very "happy". In talking about events or incidents that had made them to be sad, they talked about the fact that they were at one point in their lives bereaved or had failed a particular exam and that made them 'sad". In a situation where an informant failed to utter any of the three words earmarked for the investigation, the investigator introduced a question like "How did that make you to feel?" In that situation, the informant could not escape the targeted word the second time. The second reason for the choice of the three words was that they constituted part of the range of items through which the speech of the same informants had been evaluated in some of the phonological styles that express formality (PRS, SRS and WLS).

The recording of the informants' speech in the moods of anger, fear and joy was quite a challenging task. In order to achieve this goal, the informants, who were 4th Year Bilingual Series students at the Advanced Teachers' Training College Yaounde, were involved in a continuous assessment exercise containing words with some targeted phonological variables. The students were expected to transcribe these variables and they were made to understand that the mark they would obtain from the exercise would count for part of their evaluation for that semester.

After the first exercise, the scripts or the students' answer sheets were collected and taken away for marking. In marking the scripts, the investigator randomly selected 16 scripts and most correct answers in the selected scripts were wittingly marked wrong. This resulted in a situation where the students who were normally supposed to score, say, 14, 15 16 or any other high mark out of 20, ended up with marks below 5. When the scripts were returned to the students, those whose marks were not judiciously awarded came up very aggressively, like those who have been stung by bees, to table their complaints to the course instructor who was the investigator. They were asked to stand at least two metres away from where the investigator was sitting before presenting their complaints. With very high feelings of anger, the students concerned took turns in stating audibly which words, correctly transcribed, had been marked wrong. As the students went ahead to say which words had been marked wrong, they were unconsciously serving as informants to produce speech in the mood of anger. With the help of a hidden tape-recorder, the informants' speech in the mood of anger was recorded. It should be pointed out that asking the informants not to come too close to where the investigator was sitting (in front of the classroom) was an attempt to make them speak aloud, so that the tape-recorder could record their speech with ease.

When every student had presented his/her complaints, the course instructor (investigator) proposed to return home with the scripts in order to further re-examine them, to find out if the complaints were really genuine. During the next lesson, the course instructor returned with the scripts that were taken away in the previous lesson for re-correction. Contrary to what the students were expecting, the instructor revealed that, having re-examined all the scripts, none of the complaints actually had a genuine case. He went further to accuse the students concerned of having tampered with the scripts. He made them to understand that he suspected they had, once the scripts were returned to them after the first making, attempted the transcription of words that were not originally transcribed, just to give the impression that he had not been careful in marking the scripts. He described the crime as a criminal case which was likely to be taken up to the disciplinary council of the university if the accused students failed to convince him and the rest of the students that, they were not, in fact, guilty. At that point, the accused students saw themselves likely to be plagued by two major problems. They could end up losing the marks they knew they deserved and they could be taken up to the disciplinary council and they would spend their precious time trying to defend themselves for a crime they knew they were not guilty of.

The accused students were then expected to articulate audibly all the words that were rightly transcribed in their scripts. They needed to provide a pronunciation that matched with the correct transcription in their scripts to convince both the teacher (investigator) and the rest of the students that they mastered the pronunciation of the words correctly transcribed in their scripts. They were made to understand that this was the only way they could be awarded the marks they deserved and the only way they could avoid going to the disciplinary council. Being in a mood of fear, because of the possibility of losing their marks and being implicated at the same time, they went ahead to pronounce the words. With the help of a hidden tape-recorder, their speech was recorded again in the mood of fear. The investigator did not immediately reveal whether the students concerned had successfully defended themselves by matching their oral production with their written performance. He went back again with their scripts and it was only in the next lesson that the students were to get his reaction. It should be pointed out that at that point three students actually refused to convince the investigator and the rest of the students that they had not tampered with their scripts. This implies that the speech of the three students was not recorded in the mood of fear.

During the next lesson, the investigator brought all the scripts and started by apologising for having made false accusations against the students. He actually revealed that the students were innocent and needed to be compensated with bonus marks for being considered criminals, when in actual fact they were not. When this declaration was made, a certain mass of air, depicting happiness, could be perceived blowing through the faces of the students concerned. But this was not the case with the rest of the students who were not involved in the accusation. They were rather agitating, as they argued that it was illogical for the students involved in the accusation to be added bonus marks. As a result of this agitation, which the investigator had earlier predicted, he proposed that the accused students should go further and drill their fellow mates on all the phonological features included in the test, to prove that they, in fact, merited the high marks awarded to them. They were at the same time notified that, in case they did not succeed in providing the right articulation for the features, their marks would not be deducted and they would not equally be taken up to the disciplinary council. In other words, it was declared that the exercise of drilling their mates was just to confirm the instructor's observation that the accused students were, in fact, innocent. This notification was to enhance the experimental students' feelings of joy and to eliminate any tendency of fear in them. The persistent agitation from the non-experimental students made the investigator to declare that the students (i.e. the non-experimental students) would be given the same opportunity to provide a drill of the phonological features, after the other students had all taken turns in providing the drill, and if they succeeded in providing the right articulation for the features, they would also be given bonus marks. Everybody was satisfied with this new decision. The experimental students were very relaxed and excited in drilling their fellow mates on the phonological features. The hidden tape-recorder was used, as usual, to record their speech in the mood of excitement or joy. Two students were observed not to be very excited in drilling their mates on the phonological features. This implies that the students were not really in a mood of joy and, as a result, they were not considered as part of the sample. This therefore suggests that the total number of informants successfully evaluated in the moods of anger, fear and joy was finally reduced to 11. The other students who were not involved in the accusation were expected to take their own turns in providing the drill, in order to also benefit from the bonus marks. But immediately the accused students had provided the drill in the mood of joy, the investigator stopped the whole exercise and revealed the exact goal of it.

It is worthwhile pointing out that the study of the informants' speech in the three moods had a number of disadvantages and negative impact, both on the investigator and on the informants. On the part of the investigator, his professional image was greatly sacrificed before the aim of the exercise was ever revealed to the students. The students were tempted to believe that the investigator (teacher) did not have a good mastery of his subject matter. They could not understand, for instance, why their correct answers would be marked wrong. This made them to conclude at first that their teacher lacked professional consciousness and self confidence, especially as he expected the students to confirm their written performance by orally displaying their pronunciation skills. The process of collecting data for this dimension of the study equally had noticeable effects on the students. For instance, much of their time was sacrificed for their speech to be recorded in the moods of anger, fear and joy. Another effect was the fact that they were psychologically traumatised as the investigator wittingly set them in negative moods (fear and anger). On the whole, one cannot dispute the unethical aspects involved in the collection of data for this dimension of the study. The psychological trauma the students went through cannot, however, be over-emphasised, given that they were eventually brought to the mood of joy.

It should be noted that it was not unwitting to collect data by violating some ethical guidelines for human subjects research. The nature of data intended could not be collected without this violation. Even in the Western world where people's privacy is highly valued, there are sometimes cases of hidden video cameras being installed in suspected criminals' homes just for the truth about a crime case to be unveiled. In this case, there is the crime of violating people's privacy, but the wish to discover the truth should neutralize such a crime. In the same light, certain sociolinguistic facts will remain "hidden" if some of the prescribed rules and ethical values cannot be tampered with, especially if it is done with good intention.

3.4 Method of Data Analysis

The data collected were submitted to a simple and straight-forward analysis. A complex statistical analysis was wittingly avoided, given that the frequencies and percentages could unambiguously tell the whole story. For instance, one did not need the Chi Square to interpret a situation where approximately 95% of informants, irrespective of their social category, used the CamE variants of the linguistic variables and less than 5% uttered the Standard British English (SBE) variants, in spite of the too much emphasis on SBE in the ELT industry in Cameroon. The analysis involved a number of stages. The different pronunciations of the targeted phonological features, registered with the help of a tape-recorder, were phonetically transcribed. The transcription revealed as many as four different variants, sometimes less, for some phonological variables. The frequency of each variant for all the phonological variables was established, as far as all the non-linguistic categories are concerned. Each frequency was expressed as a percentage.

It should be reiterated again that the principal objective of analysing the data was not just to assess the degree to which the different pronunciations inherent in the speech of the informants deviate from SBE, the variety of English strongly promoted in Cameroon, but it was to determine the correlation pattern between the phonological variables and the non-linguistic variables under study. In order to determine this correlation pattern, the different pronunciations were classified into two main categories: Cameroon English (CamE) realisations and SBE realisations. Speakers were then evaluated according to the extent to which they approximated the SBE accent, the accent of the variety of English "promoted" in Cameroon. This was an attempt to determine whether the correlation patterns reported in the Western world are likely to prevail in a context with different realities.

In evaluating the extent to which speakers approximated SBE features, the frequency of each of the variants was established and the total frequency was calculated and expressed as a percentage. The different categories that make up each of the non-linguistic variables investigated were graded according to the degree to which they influenced the choice of SBE variants. For instance, as far as level of education is concerned, the three levels of education, considered in the investigation, were stratified in terms of the degree of approximation of SBE variants. The other sociolinguistic variables were evaluated in the same manner, except in the case of regionality where speakers were not only evaluated in terms of their approximation to SBE, but also in terms of the degree of diversity in their speech. The different phonological styles and the different moods considered in the investigation were also analysed in terms of the extent to which they influenced the choice of SBE variants.

Chapter Four
Correlation Patterns in Cameroon

4. Introduction

This chapter presents the correlation between the different non-linguistic variables under study and English phonological variables in Cameroon, a New English context that continues to target SBE. Through the analysis of the data collected, Cameroon-style correlation patterns clearly emerge. In the next sections, these patterns will be presented and discussed in detail and it would be demonstrated whether such patterns reflect what has been reported in the Western world, a context that has realities different from those of Cameroon.

4.1 Educationally-Based Correlation in Cameroon

The principal concern of this section is the question of whether in Cameroon English linguistic variables correlate substantially with level of education. In order to determine this correlation, speakers selected according to their level of education were evaluated in terms of the degree of approximation of SBE pronunciation, the accent claimed to be the target in the Cameroonian classroom. As pointed out in the last chapter, secondary school students, undergraduate and postgraduate students were evaluated in different phonological styles according to the extent to which they approximated the SBE pronunciation of the 102 linguistic items considered in the investigation.

The frequencies and the corresponding percentages of the various variants (see Appendix 2) revealed two different patterns of correlation between English phonological variables and the three levels of education. The first pattern shows a situation where no considerable correlation emerged between the linguistic variables and the levels of education. The second pattern shows a situation where there is seemingly a substantial correlation, though this is still far below what is obtained in a mother tongue English context. Each of the patterns would be examined in greater detail.

Linguistic variables without a substantial correlation with the levels of education (secondary school students (S), undergraduate students (U) and postgraduate students (P)) are displayed in table 4a below.

Table 4a: Linguistic variables showing no substantial correlation with level of education

Items	SBE	CamE	S %	U %	P %
	Variants				
c*a*t	c[æ]t		0	2	0
		c[a]t	100	98	100
p*e*riod	p[ɪə]riod		0	1	0
		p[i]riod	100	99	100
		p[ie]riod	0	0	0
o*f*	o[v]		0	0	0
		o[f]	100	100	100
Jo*s*eph	Jo[z]eph		0	0	0
		Jo[s]eph	100	100	100
re*s*ide	re[z]ide		0	2	0
		re[s]ide	100	98	100
diversified	d'iversified		0	0	0
		diversi'fied	99	88	0
		'diversified	1	12	0
however	how'ever		0	1	0
		'however	100	99	100
preparatory	pre'paratory		0	1	0
		prepa'ratory	100	99	100
authoritative	au'thoritative		0	1	0
		authori'tative	100	99	100
explanatory	ex'planatory		0	1	0
		expla'natory	100	99	100
commented	'commented		0	1	0
		com'mented	100	99	100
illogical	il'logical		0	1	0
		'illogical	100	99	100
insurance	in'surance		1	2	0
		'insurance	99	98	100
irrelevant	ir'relevant		0	2	0
		'irrelevant	100	98	100

The first column of the above table displays the different linguistic items that did not show any considerable correlation with the levels of education. The second column shows the SBE variants for each of the linguistic variables and the third column captures the CamE variants. The percentages of the different variants in the speech of the three groups of students are displayed in the fourth, fifth and sixth columns respectively. As the above table shows, the linguistic items on which the informants were evaluated involve segments and stress. In the realisation of these linguistic items, no substantial correlation emerged in the way speakers approximated the SBE variants of the linguistic variables. The SBE variants were almost absent in the speech of the speakers, irrespective of level of education (see Appendix 2 for more details). Interestingly, mainstream CamE features dominated the speech of most of the informants, as the table shows.

In spite of the cases displayed in table 4a, which involve no considerable correlation between level of education and the linguistic variables evaluated, a good number of the linguistic items fairly correlated with the speakers' level of education. Table 4b below captures such linguistic items. The different linguistic items, the SBE variants and the CamE variants are respectively presented in the first, second and third columns. The scores of secondary school students, undergraduate students and postgraduate students are displayed in the fourth, fifth and sixth columns respectively.

Table 4b: Linguistic variables showing a remarkable correlation with level of education

Items	SBE	CamE	S %	U %	P %
pool	p[uː]l		13	40	52
		p[u]l	87	60	48
pull	p[ʊ]l		7	37	39
		p[u]l	93	63	61
pestle	pes[ø]le		11	49	72
		pes[t]le	89	51	28
castle	cas[ø]le		4	44	62
		cas[t]le	96	56	38
satan	s[eɪ]tan		1	16	28
		s[a]tan	99	80	59
		s[ɛ]tan	0	4	13
legal	l[iː]gal		2	17	31
		l[e]gal	98	83	69
penal	p[iː]nal		2	14	24
		p[e]nal	91	83	67
		p[ɛ]nal	7	3	9
Joan	J[əʊ]n		0	22	31
		J[ɔa]n	100	78	69
combat	ˈcombat		0	13	24
		comˈbat	100	87	76
ancestor	ˈancestor		1	6	25
		anˈcestor	99	64	75
referee	refeˈree		67	38	33
		ˈreferee	23	62	67
Vivian	ˈVivian		2	35	33
		Viˈvian	98	65	67
Eunice	ˈEunice		5	49	59
		Euˈnice	95	51	41

As can be seen from the table above, there is a remarkable increase in the use of SBE features as one climbs the educational ladder. In linguistic items that simply involve the distinction between long and short sounds, the correlation pattern tends to be fairly substantial. In the articulation of the vowels of the words *pool* and *pull,* for instance, the percentages of SBE realisations in the speech of secondary school students stands at 13% and 7% respectively. In the realisation of the same linguistic variables, undergraduate students' scores are as high as 40% and 37% respectively. The highest scores characterise the speech of postgraduate students who score 52% and 39% respectively. This fair correlation is observable in most linguistic items that simply involve the distinction between long and short vowels.

Besides the linguistic items involving the distinction between long and short sounds, there is equally a considerable correlation between the levels of education and the other linguistic items involving segments and stress, as the percentage of SBE features remarkably increases in the speech of speakers with a higher level of education. For instance, the realization of the diphthong of the word "satan" fairly correlates with the informants' level of education. The italicised grapheme of the word is realised as a diphthong in SBE, but in CamE, it is either realised as /a/ or /ɛ/. The percentage of the SBE pronunciation in the speech of secondary school students is just one percent and this sharply contrasts with the scores of 16% and 28% which characterize the speech of undergraduate and postgraduate students, respectively. The CamE variants /a/ and /ɛ/ equally tend to correlate remarkably with the speakers' level of education. As high as 99% of the variant [a] characterizes the speech of secondary school students. The percentage of this pronunciation, which tends to reflect the general pattern in Cameroon, reduces to 80% in the speech of undergraduate students and to 59% in the speech of postgraduate students. This is an indication that more educational attainment rather takes speakers away from mainstream CamE pronunciation. The other pronunciation, s[ɛ]*tan*, which is a reduction of the SBE variant [eɪ] and somewhat closer to it than [a], also tends to be graded according to the speakers' level of education. The percentage of this variant is zero in the speech of secondary school students, 4% in the speech of undergraduate students and 13% in the speech of postgraduate students. The occurrence of /ɛ/, and not [a], in the speech of a handful of undergraduate and postgraduate students suggests a conscious effort on their part to approximate the SBE variant [eɪ]. The complete absence of /ɛ/ in the speech of secondary school students and the fact that only a single secondary school student successfully uses the SBE variant [eɪ] suggests that their level of education has not yet exposed them to the SBE pronunciation of the word.

The fair correlation that characterizes the pronunciation of the word "satan", discussed above, is observable in most of the linguistic items involving both segments and stress. But the realisation of the stress pattern of the word "referee" shows a pattern of correlation that rather contrasts with what is obtained with the other linguistic variables. The word, like most of the words that have the ending *ee*, follows a forward-stress pattern in SBE as is primarily stressed on the final syllable to yield *refe'ree*. Ironically, this variant (the SBE variant) tends to be more frequent in the speech of secondary school students than in the speech of university students. The percentage of this variant stands at 67% in the speech of secondary school students, as the table clearly shows, and this contrasts with the scores of 38% and 33% which characterize the speech of undergraduate and postgraduate students respectively. This tendency can be explained by the fact that speakers with a low educational attainment, like secondary school students, tend to be "caught up" in the general stress pattern of CamE, which, generally speaking, favors a forward-stress pattern and in this situation, they unwittingly approximate the stress pattern of the word, as obtained in SBE. It is for this reason that most of the undergraduate and postgraduate students stressed the word on the first syllable as *'referee*.

The patterns of correlation between the levels of education and the linguistic variables discussed above do not present the overall picture as far as all the linguistic variables are concerned. In order to determine this overall picture, the total average percentage of SBE variants was calculated in the speech of the three categories of speakers, as far as all the linguistic variables evaluated are concerned. The results showed that the total average percentage of SBE pronunciation stood at 4.69% in the speech of secondary school students (speakers with the lowest level of education). As concerns undergraduate and postgraduate students, the total average percentage of SBE features in their speech stood at 12.12% and 17.85% respectively, scores substantially higher than that of secondary school students. The substantial difference between the scores of secondary school students and those of undergraduate and postgraduate students is generally accounted for by the fact that a lot of efforts is made at the university level to teach SBE pronunciation, though these efforts do not always yield the expected results. The scores of the three categories of speakers are captured in the following bar chart:

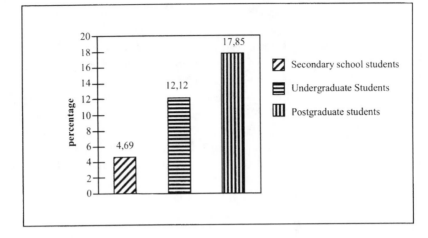

Figure 2: Total average percentage of SBE features in the speech of secondary school, undergraduate and postgraduate students

As the chart shows, level of education seems to show a considerable correlation with linguistic variables. It should be acknowledged that, in spite of the seemingly remarkable correlation that emerges between the speakers' level of education and linguistic variables, the degree of approximation of SBE, the variety of English taught and promoted in Cameroon, is still far below expectation, especially if the situation is compared to what has been reported in the Western world. A number of reasons can be advanced to explain why SBE linguistic features tend to be very lacking in the speech of Cameroonian speakers of English, irrespective of educational attainment. The first reason is the fact that the English language in Cameroon is significantly rooted in the socio-cultural realities of the place and, as a result, pedagogic efforts cannot easily neutralize the twists and turns the language has undergone in Cameroon.

The second reason, which has been raised in previous studies, is the attitude towards speakers who strive to approximate a mother tongue English accent in Cameroon. If speakers of a mother tongue English accent are often looked upon with contempt rather than admiration, then such an attitude is likely to have tremendous consequences on pedagogic efforts to promote such a variety of English. In fact, there is likely to be a tendency where speakers may make a conscious effort to restrict their speech, as much as possible, to the local accent, in order to avoid inviting negative impressions about them. In this case, the official objective to teach and promote the native English accent is likely to be weakened by such an attitude.

The third reason is what previous scholars (e. g. Kachru, 1986 and Bobda, 2000b) have referred to as the colonial input. It is argued that the English language inherited from earlier European settlers was substandard English. Kachru (1986:22) and Bobda (2000b: 4), in fact, argue that the colonial masters did not wish to teach their language too well to the colonised since they wanted to maintain a distance between the rulers and the ruled. It should be emphasized here that most of the earlier European settlers, as current literature shows, were not even native speakers of English. In the particular case of Cameroon, the Portuguese were the first European settlers and since then, various Europeans such as the Spaniards, the Dutch, the Germans, and the English have lived and worked in Cameroon for various reasons. In such a situation, Cameroonian speakers of English have been introduced to a wide range of English accents, most of which are not standard accents of English.

The linguistic landscape of Cameroon provides the fourth reason. In a complex linguistic landscape like Cameroon where, besides French and English as the official languages and Pidgin English as the lingua franca, there are approximately 280 local languages, no mother English accent is likely to dominate the speech of the speakers. The SBE accent is, in fact, in competition with a multitude of accents in Cameroon and this partly explains why the percentage of SBE features in the speech of the informants turns out to be very low, irrespective of their educational level.

The quality of English taught to Cameroonian learners constitutes the fifth reason why the realisation of native English features tends to be very low in the speech of the informants of this study in particular and Cameroonian speakers of English in general. At the secondary school level, for instance, English is taught by those whose speech is almost a complete deviation from mother tongue English accent. Some of the teachers may not have had the opportunity to listen to a typical speaker of RP or may not even have interacted meaningfully with traditional native speakers. In such a situation, one cannot expect the teachers concerned to teach, with any high degree of effectiveness, an accent that is psychologically, physically and practically cut off from them. In such a situation, a high educational attainment cannot guarantee a significant approximation of SBE by Cameroonian speakers of English.

The last reason is the inconsistency between spelling and pronunciation. Sometimes it is difficult to understand why the *s* of the word "visitor" and "nursery" should have different phonological realisations, as that of the former is voiced and that of the latter is voiceless. One equally needs much time to understand why the *e* of "penal" and "legal", for instance, is phonologically realised as [iː], and not as [ɛ] or [e] as in 'pen", "met", and "allege". This inconsistency between spelling and pronunciation sometimes misleads speakers of the New Englishes. One may not be altogether wrong to predict that a more striking correlation between level of education and linguistic variables would have emerged if speakers were evaluated in terms of their approximation of

"Standard" CamE features. But it should be noted that there is yet to be a consensus on what should actually constitute Cameroon Standard English.

4.2 Gender-Based Correlation in Cameroon

In almost all gender-based linguistic investigations underscored in §2.2, there is a well established view that male and female speakers have linguistic differences and, in this situation, women are associated more with prestige or standard forms of speech. What is likely to be the pattern of correlation in a context such as Cameroon, which has linguistic and socio-cultural realities very different from those of communities where female-male linguistic differences have been previously investigated? In fact, besides being a context where English is not used as a mother tongue, Cameroon presents a situation where speakers of an Inner Circle accent are sometimes looked upon with contempt. Given this type of situation, if it is a natural gift that women should always use more prestige forms of speech than men, what is likely to be their target in the Cameroonian context? Would they strive to approximate phonological features of an Inner Circles English and be condemned or would they strive to use features of the local accent and lose the privilege that women in, say, the UK have always enjoyed by approximating features of Standard British English? Given that what should constitute the norm within Cameroon English, especially at the level of pronunciation, is still to be determined, what should women in such a context strive to approximate if they want to enjoy the same privilege women in traditional native English contexts enjoy for approximating standard English features? What linguistic choices are women in Cameroon likely to make in the face of this type of situation?

The analysis of the data revealed two types of correlation patterns. The first one involves a situation where the realisation of the SBE variants of a good number of linguistic items tends to show no substantial difference between male and female speakers, at both segmental and supra-segmental levels. The second one, and probably a more interesting one, involves a situation where women tend to show an "advantage" over men in the use of variants that are neither those of mainstream CamE nor those of any mother tongue English accent. As concerns the first correlation pattern, there was no remarkable difference in the way female and male speakers articulated many of the linguistic items evaluated. In this situation, two other tendencies could be observed. The first one involves a situation where no single informant from the two gender categories successfully used the SBE variants of certain linguistic items and the second tendency shows that some speakers, at least, approximated the SBE variants, but the scores are not substantially graded according to the gender of the speakers.

The following table vividly presents the first situation, where no single informant used the SBE variants of a number of linguistic features, irrespective of their gender category.

Table 4c: Linguistic items showing a complete absence of the SBE variants in the speech of male and female speakers

Items	Variants		Male speakers	Female speakers
	SBE	CamE	%	%
village	vill[ɪ]ge		0	0
		vill[e]ge	100	100
of	o[v]		0	0
		o[f]	100	100
conserve	con[s]erve		0	0
		con[z]erve	0	0
Joseph	Jo[z]eph		0	0
		Jo[s]eph	100	100
commented	'commented		0	0
		com'mented	100	100
embarrass	em'barrass		0	0
		embar'rass	100	100
however	how'ever		0	0
		'however	100	100
irrelevant	ir'relevant		0	0
		'irrelevant	100	100
jubilee	'jubilee		0	0
		jubi'lee	100	100

The first column presents the linguistic items that showed a complete absence in the speech of the two categories of speakers. The second and third columns respectively display the SBE and the CamE variants of the linguistic variables. The fourth and fifth columns show the percentages of the variants in the speech of male and female speakers, respectively. As can be seen from the table, no informant, irrespective of his or her gender category, approximated the SBE variants of all the linguistic items displayed. As concerns the linguistic items: "village", "of", "conserve", and "Joseph" which involve segments, the speech of both male and female speakers was characterised by the CamE variants: "vill[e]ge", "o[f]", "con[z]erve" and "Jo[s]eph". As the table shows, the same situation is equally observed in all linguistic items that involve stress. No informant, regardless of their gender group, successfully stressed the words *commented, embarrass, however, irrelevant* and *jubilee* as they are realised in SBE. Instead of 'commented, em'barrass how'ever, ir'relevant and 'jubilee, all the informants realised the CamE variants as com'mented, embar'rass, how'ever, ir'relevant and jubi'lee respectively. Besides the fact that the data show no difference at all between the speech of male and female speakers, they have the sociolinguistic importance of revealing the systematic nature of CamE features.

As earlier pointed out, a few speakers, at least, approximated the SBE variants of some of the linguistic variables, but the scores do not show any considerable correlation between male and female speech. Such linguistic features are captured in the table below.

Table 4d: Male and female speakers showing no substantial difference in approximating some SBE features involving segments

Items	Variants		Male speakers	Female speakers
	SBE	**CamE**	**%**	**%**
drugs	dr[ʌ]gs		1.98	1.98
		dr[ɔ]gs	98	98
Joan	ʃ[əʊ]n		6.6	7.3
		ʃ[ɔa]n	93.3	92.7
said	sai[d]		0.7	1.3
		sai[t]	99.3	98.7
dog	do[g]		1.98	2.64
		do[k]	98	97.35
basic	ba[s]ic		5.3	5.96
		ba[z]ic	94.7	94
singing	si[ŋiŋ]		0.7	1.98
		si[ngin]	99.3	98
bosom	b[ʊ]som		1.3	0
		b[ɔ]som	98.7	100
castle	cas[ø]le		24.5	25.82
		cas[t]le	75.49	74.17
tour	t[ʊə]		1.98	0.7
		t[ɔ]	98	99.3
visitor	vi[z]itor		1.3	0
		vi[s]itor	98.7	100

As can be seen from the table, in the pronunciation of the linguistic variables displayed in the table, the percentages of SBE variants do not show any striking difference between the pronunciations of male and female speakers.

There are equally a number of linguistic items at the level of stress, which display a correlation pattern similar to the one captured in the above table. The following table displays such linguistic items.

Table 4e: Male and female speakers showing no remarkable difference in approximating some SBE features involving stress

Items	Variants		Male speakers	Female speakers
	SBE	CamE	%	%
combat	'combat		4.6	5.3
		com'bat	95.4	94.7
interesting	'interesting		2.65	2.65
		inte'resting	97.35	97.35
challenging	'challenging		0	0.7
		chal'lenging	100	99.3
biased	'biased		0	0.7
		bi'ased	100	99.3
favouritism	'favouritism		0	0.7
		favou'ritism	100	99.3
insurance	in'surance		0.7	0
		'insurance	99.3	100
illogical	il'logical		0.7	0
		'illogical	99.3	100
preparatory	pre'paratory		0.7	0
		prepa'ratory	99.3	100
explanatory	ex'planatory		0.7	0
		expla'natory	99.3	100
authoritative	au'thoritative		0.7	0
		authori'tative	99.3	100

Unlike those linguistic items earlier discussed, where no single informant successfully approximated the SBE stress pattern of the words, the table above shows linguistic items involving stress where some speakers actually approximated the SBE stress pattern, but the scores do not show any substantial correlation with the gender of the speakers. The CamE variants dominated the speech of most of the informants, as the table shows.

In spite of the numerous linguistic items discussed above that show no substantial correlation with the gender of the speakers, the SBE variants of a few linguistic items appear to be considerably graded according to the gender of the speakers. This situation is seen in the way the speakers articulated the SBE stress pattern of proper nouns, such as, "Vivian", "Eunice" and "Helen" (see Appendix 3 for details).

In addition to the correlation patterns discussed above, female speakers showed an edge over male speakers in the use of variants that are neither those of mainstream CamE nor those of any mother tongue English accent. This tendency is captured in the table below.

Table 4f: Female speakers showing an edge over male speakers in the use of variants that are neither those of mainstream CamE nor those of any mother tongue English accent

Items	Variants		Male speakers	Female speakers
	SBE	CamE	%	%
cupboard	cupb[ɔ]d		1.98	1.32
		cupb[ɔ]d	98	94
		cupb[ʌ]d	0	4.6
period	p[ɪ]riod		0.7	0
		p[i]riod	99.3	97.4
		p[ie]riod	0	2.6
satan	s[eɪ]tan		5.29	5.96
		s[a]tan	91.39	82.11
		s[ɛ]tan	3.3	11.9
aren't	[ɑːnt]		0.7	5.29
		[arent]	7.3	13.24
		[arənt]	92	88
diversified	di'versified		0	0
		diversi'fied	100	92.7
		'diversified	0	7.3

The first column of the table displays linguistic items whose variants are neither those of mainstream CamE nor those of any native English accent. The second and third columns respectively display SBE and CamE variants. The percentages of the variants in the speech of male and female speakers are presented in the fourth and fifth columns respectively. Those variants that neither reflect mainstream CamE nor any mother tongue English are highlighted. Interestingly, these variants are more dominant in the speech of female speakers than in the speech of their male counterparts, as table 4f above shows. The SBE variants, like the cases previously discussed, do not show any considerable correlation with the different gender categories.

The implication is that women in Cameroon, like those in other communities where male–female linguistic differences have been investigated, wish to sound differently from their male counterparts, but the realities of Cameroon make it difficult for such a wish to be fulfilled. They are caught up in the dilemma of what really constitutes prestige English linguistic features in Cameroon. If SBE features or features of another mother tongue variety of English are associated with prestige and those of CamE are considered stigmatized, then the question is: how many Cameroonians, including the female speakers themselves, have a good mastery of British English? It should be noted that some of such features that characterized female speech are very close to SBE variants, but are still significantly different. For example, the variant 'diversified is very close to SBE variant di'versified in the sense that they all display a backward stress pattern, though the SBE variant is one syllable less backward than the hyper-corrected variant found in female speech. The hyper-corrected variant *'diversified* is, interestingly, very different from mainstream CamE variant, *diversi'fied.* This implies that if SBE features or those of any mother tongue English were very accessible to Cameroonian speakers of English, women in Cameroon may likely choose such features in order to enjoy the privilege that women in other places enjoy for approximating standard or prestige linguistic features. But Cameroonians who make a conscious effort to use such linguistic features are rather ridiculed than admired (see Mbangwana 1987). In such a situation, Cameroonian female speakers wishing to sound differently from their male counterparts, especially at the level of pronunciation, only end up producing features which are neither reflecting mainstream CamE nor any native English.

It should however be noted that if Cameroonians develop a more positive attitude towards their variety of English and re-orientate ELT goals towards the local variety of English, educated CamE features may easily acquire the prestige always associated with SBE features. In this case, female speakers interested in approximating prestige linguistic features can easily make linguistic choices from the local linguistic repertoire, instead of targeting SBE features and missing them.

The discussion underscored so far in §4.2 presents the different correlation patterns that emerged between linguistic variables and the gender categories. In order to determine whether there was any substantial correlation between the gender categories and the SBE variants of all the linguistic items evaluated, the total average percentage of SBE variants in the speech of male and female speakers was calculated. Interestingly, the percentage of SBE features in the speech of female speakers stood at 4.56% and that of male speakers was 4.64%, as captured in the following bar-chart.

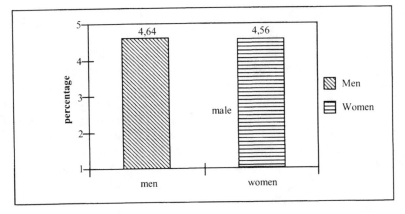

Figure 3: Percentage of SBE features in the speech of male and female speakers

The scores displayed in the above chart shows no difference between male and female speech in terms of the approximation of features of SBE, the variety of English associated with prestige and the variety assumed to be the target in ELT in Cameroon.

4.3 Age-Based Correlation in Cameroon

If gender is not instrumental in determining prestige variants of the variety of English that is targeted in the ELT industry in Cameroon, as demonstrated in the last section, what is likely to be the pattern of correlation between age and linguistic variables? Following the analysis of the speech of 200 informants in Word List style, selected according to four different age groups, two correlation patterns emerged. The first one shows a tendency, as observed in the cases of level of education and gender, whereby no substantial correlation emerged between the SBE variants of many of the linguistic variables evaluated and age, irrespective of the age group. The second correlation pattern involves a tendency whereby the SBE variants of certain linguistic items were considerably graded according to the age group of the speakers. Each of the correlation patterns would be discussed below in greater detail.

The linguistic variables whose SBE variants were completely absent in the speech of the informants, irrespective of the age group, are presented in the following table.

Table 4g: Linguistic items showing a complete absence of the SBE variants in the speech of the different age groups

Items	Variants		12-19 years	20-30 years	31-49 years	Above 49 years
	SBE	CamE	%	%	%	%
period	p[ɪə]riod		0	0	0	0
		p[i]riod	100	98	84	98
		p[ie]riod	0	2	16	2
of	o[v]		0	0	0	0
		o[f]	100	100	100	100
jubilee	'jubilee		0	0	0	0
		jubi'lee	100	100	100	100

The first column of the table displays linguistic variables whose SBE variants were completely absent in the speech of the different age groups. The second and third columns respectively present the SBE and CamE variants of the linguistic variables. The percentages of the different variants in the speech of the age groups are displayed in the rest of the columns. The table shows that no single informant, irrespective of the age group articulated the SBE variants of the linguistic variables. One can also notice that mainstream CamE variants dominated the speech of the speakers and a few speakers exhibited a pronunciation feature that is neither that of CamE nor that of any native English, as seen in the case of "p[ie]riod". Such a pronunciation pattern signals the presence of female speakers in the sample, given that such pronunciation features were demonstrated in the last section to be peculiar of women's speech.

Besides the linguistic items examined above, which show that the CamE variants dominated the speech of all the informants, irrespective of their age groups, there are equally a number of linguistic items, both at the levels of segments and stress, which did not show any substantial correlation with the speakers' age, but a few informants, at least, used the SBE variants. The table below displays such linguistic items.

Table 4b: Linguistic variables showing no remarkable correlation with the different age groups.

Items	Variants		12-19 years	20-30 years	31-49 years	Above 49 years
	SBE	CamE	%	%	%	%
village	vill[ɪ]ge		0	0	0	2
		vill[e]ge	100	100	100	98
bosom	b[ʊ]som		0	0	4	0
		b[ɔ]som	100	100	96	100
Joseph	Jo[z]eph		0	0	2	0
		Jo[s]eph	100	100	98	100
happy	h[æ]ppy		0	0	2	0
		h[a]ppy	100	100	98	100
commented	'commented		0	0	2	0
		com'mented	100	100	98	100
illogical	il'logical		0	0	2	0
		'illogical	100	100	98	100
however	how'ever		0	0	2	0
		'however	100	100	98	100
insurance	in'surance		0	0	2	0
		'insurance	100	100	98	100
preparatory	pre'paratory		0	0	2	0
		prepa'ratory	100	100	98	100
explanatory	ex'planatory		0	0	2	0
		expla'natory	100	100	98	100
authoritative	au'thoritative		0	0	2	0
		authori'tative	100	100	98	100

In spite of the numerous instances of lack of a substantial correlation between the linguistic variables and the different age groups discussed above, there are a number of linguistic items, which fairly correlate with age. In the articulation of such linguistic items, captured in the table below, there is a noticeable increase in the use of SBE variants as one climbs the age ladder, though in some cases there are unexpected patterns.

Table 4i: Linguistic variables showing a remarkable correlation with the different age groups

Items	Variants SBE	CamE	12-19 years %	20-30 years %	31-49 years %	Above 49 years %
legal	l[i:]gal		10	14	22	20
		l[e]al	90	86	78	80
penal	p[i:]nal		0	2	10	6
		p[e]nal	96	94	80	70
		p[ɛ]nal	4	4	10	24
castle	cas[ø]le		36	48	58	50
		cas[t]le	64	52	42	50
pestle	pes[ø]le		12	28	66	36
		pes[t]le	88	72	34	64
interesting	'interesting		0	2	8	14
		inter'esting	100	98	92	86
referee	refe'ree		36	2	2	22
		'referee	64	98	98	78

The linguistic items that show a substantial correlation with age are presented in the first column. The second and third columns respectively display the different SBE and CamE variants of the linguistic variables. The rest of the columns present the percentage scores of the different age groups. Most of the linguistic items displayed in the above table show a noticeable increase in the use of SBE features, though this increase is still far below what could obtain if the informants were evaluated in terms of the standard features of their local variety of English.

The discussion so far in this section underscores two main correlation patterns. The first one presents linguistic items that do not show any considerable correlation with the age of the speakers. The second pattern involves a tendency where the approximation of the SBE variants of some linguistic items is substantially graded according to the age group of the speakers, given that the SBE variants tends to be more frequent in the speech of older speakers than in the speech of younger speakers, though there are some exceptional cases (see the case of the word "referee", for instance). But these patterns do not present the overall picture of age-based correlation in Cameroon, given that the correlation between linguistic variables and the different age groups, underscored so far in this section, is far from being uniform. Do older speakers actually use more "standard" forms of speech than younger speakers?

In order to determine whether older speakers in Cameroon use more "standard" forms of speech (SBE features in the case of Cameroon) than younger speakers as far as all the linguistic variables are concerned, the total average percentage of SBE features in the speech of the different age groups was calculated. The results show that the total average percentage of SBE features was 4% in the speech of speakers between the ages of 12 and 19; 6.68% in the speech of speakers between the ages of 20 and 30; 10.7% in the speech of speakers between 31 and 49 years and 8.68% in the speech of speakers above the age of 49. These scores are captured in the following graph.

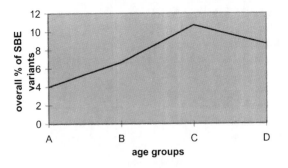

Figure 4: Age-based correlation in Cameroon

As can be seen from the graph above, the approximation of SBE features depends to a certain extent on the age of the speakers. The lowest percentage of SBE variants was scored by speakers between 12 and 19 (A) (the youngest age group) and the highest percentage of the SBE variants was scored by speakers between 31 and 49 (C) (the age group next to the oldest group). These scores are reflected in the shape of the graph which steadily rises from left to right, as one moves progressively from one age group to another. The only exception is the score of speakers above the age of 49 (D), which interrupts the steady rising of the curve. But the score of this group of speakers, though lower than that of speakers between 31 and 49 years, is still higher than that of the other age groups.

The correlation pattern that emerges from this investigation between linguistic variables and age is very similar to Chambers' (1995) age-based correlation pattern underscored in §2.5. But the reasons which account for Chambers' correlation pattern tend to be very different from those that account for the pattern established in this study. According to Chambers (ibid.), as earlier pointed out, it is as a result of the rebellious tendency of young speakers that they distance themselves from the standard linguistic features of the older generation. This explanation would convincingly account, in a context like Cameroon, for an age-based correlation pattern whose linguistic scope is limited to the lexico-syntactic level. In Cameroon, the younger generation, especially the youths, has the tendency to establish a linguistic identity, as observed in

Chambers' society. But such a tendency is manifested more concretely at the lexico-syntactic level than at any other linguistic level, given that Cameroonian youths can easily be identified with a specialised vocabulary. But at the level of pronunciation, the situation is very different. The fact that younger speakers were discovered to be more distant from SBE phonological features than older speakers cannot be seen as a conscious attempt to create a linguistic identity, as could be the case at the lexico-syntactic level. The tendency can rather be explained from the perspective of the speakers' educational attainment. In fact, the age-based correlation pattern that emerges in this work is more of a consequence of difference in level of education than being a consequence of difference in age. Younger speakers tend to have a lower percentage of SBE features than older speakers because their level of education has not enabled them to be exposed to SBE features in the same degree as older speakers. In the unique case of speakers between the ages of 31 and 49, the percentage of SBE features tends to be higher than that of the age group above them. But the explanation, as earlier pointed out, is still related to the difference in level of education. In fact, there were a good number of informants above the age of 49 who had not received university education, where a lot of energy and efforts are sacrificed to expose students to features of SBE, though this not always done with much success.

4.4 Occupationally-Based Correlation in Cameroon (Effects of Market Pressures)

As pointed out in the previous chapter, a speaker's occupation is studied in this work in terms of "market pressures". The principal aim of this section is to establish the extent to which journalists and secondary school teachers of English are influenced by market pressures to use more SBE features than teachers of other disciplines and medical doctor who are relatively less concerned with "Standard English". Through an evaluation of the speech of 15 informants per occupational group, the correlation pattern between occupation and linguistic variables was obtained (see Appendix 5). Like the cases of the other sociolinguistic variables previously discussed, the analysis revealed different tendencies. One of the tendencies involves a situation where a number of linguistic items do not correlate remarkably with the different occupational groups. The second tendency shows a situation where many SBE variants characterized the speech of journalists and secondary school teachers of English.

As concerns the first tendency involving no considerable correlation between linguistic variables and the different occupational groups, two types of tendencies were identified. The first tendency shows a situation where no informant, irrespective of occupational status, used the SBE variants of a number of linguistic items, as seen in tables 4j and 4i below.

Table 4j: Linguistic variables involving SBE variants completely lacking in the speech of all the informants, irrespective of their occupational group

Items	Variants		Teachers of English %	Medical doctors %	Teachers of other disciplines %	Journalists %
	SBE	CamE				
cupboard	cupb[ə]d		0	0	0	0
		cupb[ɔ]d	86.7	100	100	66.7
		cupb[ʌ]d	13.3	0	0	33.3
of	o[v]		0	0	0	0
		o[f]	100	100	100	100
period	p[ɪə]riod		0	0	0	0
		p[i]riod	93.3	100	100	100
		p[ie]riod	6.7	0	0	0
village	vill[ɪ]ge		0	0	0	0
		vill[e]ge	100	100	100	100
happy	h[æ]ppy		0	0	0	0
		h[a]ppy	100	100	100	100

The above table shows that all the informants used the CamE variants of the linguistic variables and the SBE variants were completely lacking in their speech.

At the level of stress, there are equally a number of linguistic items whose SBE variants were not realised at all by any informant, regardless of the influence of market pressures, as the following table shows.

Table 4k: Linguistic items involving the SBE stress variants that were completely lacking in the speech of all the informant, regardless of occupational group

Items	Variants		Teachers of English %	Medical doctors %	Teachers of other disciplines %	Journalists %
	SBE	CamE				
commented	'commented		0	0	0	0
		com'mented	100	100	100	100
insurance	in'surance		0	0	0	0
		'insurance	100	100	100	100
illogical	il'logical		0	0	0	0
		'illogical	100	100	100	100
preparatory	pre'paratory		0	0	0	0
		prepa'ratory	100	100	100	100
explanatory	ex'planatory		0	0	0	0

The above table shows that the CamE variants dominated the speech of all the informants and no single informant used the SBE variants, irrespective of the occupational group. There are linguistic variables whose SBE variants were, at least, approximated by a few informants, but the scores were not substantially graded according to the different occupational groups (see Appendix 5 for a full range of such linguistic items).

In spite of the numerous cases involving no considerable correlation between linguistic variables and the occupational groups, a number of linguistic variables involving segments and stress correlated considerably with the occupational groups, as tables 4l and 4m illustrate.

Table 4l: Linguistic items involving segments showing a remarkable correlation with the different occupational groups

	Variants		Teachers of English	Medical doctors	Teachers of other disciplines	Journalists
Items	SBE	CamE	%	%	%	%
recent	r[iː]cent		40	20	26.7	53.3
		r[e]cent	53.3	80	73.3	40
		r[ɛ]cent	6.7	0	0	6.7
castle	cas[ø]le		86.7	40	53.3	100
		cas[t]le	13.3	60	46.7	0
pestle	pes[ø]le		73.3	33.3	33.3	93.3
		pes[t]le	26.7	66.7	66.7	6.7
journalist	journalis[t]		100	20	73.3	100
		journalis[ø]	0	80	26.7	0
typist	typis[t]		80	26.7	46.7	100
		typis[ø]	20	73.3	53.3	0
first	firs[t]		73.3	26.7	60	93.3
		firs[ø]	26.7	73.3	40	6.7

The above table shows linguistic items involving segments which correlate considerably with the different occupational groups. It can be noticed from the table that the SBE variants of all the linguistic variables are conspicuously higher in the speech of journalists and teachers of English than in the speech of medical doctors and teachers of disciplines other than English.

At the level of stress, there are equally a number of cases where the SBE variants tend to be more dominant in the speech of journalists and teachers of English than in the speech of medical doctors and teachers of other disciplines, as shown in the following table.

Table 4m: Linguistic variables involving stress showing a substantial correlation with occupational groups

Items	SBE	CamE	Teachers of English %	Medical doctors %	Teachers of other disciplines %	Journalists %
Colleague	'colleague		20	0	6.7	33.3
		col'league	80	100	93.3	66.7
success	suc'cess		26.7	0	0	26.7
		'success	73.3	100	100	73.3
interesting	'interesting		26.7	133	0	46.7
		inte'resting	73.3	86.7	100	53.3
classified	'classified		26.7	13.3	6.7	46.7
		classi'fied	73.3	86.7	93.3	53.3
satisfied	'satisfied		33.3	13.3	0	60
		satis'fied	66.7	86.7	100	40
criticised	'criticised		46.7	20	13.3	60
		criti'cised	53.3	80	86.7	40
journalism	'journalism		26.7	6.7	0	60
		jour'n-alism	73.3	93.3	100	40
Vivian	'Vivian		46.7	6.7	13.3	73.3
		Vi'vian	53.3	93.3	86.7	26.7
Eunice	'Eunice		60	20	20	80
		Eu'nice	40	80	80	20
Helen	'Helen		73.3	33.3	20	66.7
		He'len	26.7	66.7	80	33.3

It can also be noticed from the table that, besides the fact that the percentages of SBE variants are higher in the speech of journalists and teachers of English, teachers of disciplines other than English also tend to show a considerable edge over medical doctors in the approximation of SBE variants.

It should be noted at this point that the different tendencies, underscored so far, do not show an overall picture of the extent to which each occupational group approximated the SBE variants of all the linguistic variables evaluated. For instance, some linguistic variables showed a considerable correlation with the occupational groups and some did not. In such a situation, one cannot easily say whether in the overall assessment, journalists and teachers of English, who are under the influence of market pressures, actually used more SBE features than medical doctors and teachers of other disciplines, who have relatively little to do with speech. In order to determine this overall picture, the total average percentage of SBE variants was calculated. It was revealed that the percentage of SBE variants, as far as all the linguistic variables evaluated are concerned, stood at 27.5% in the speech of journalists; 20% in the speech of secondary school teachers of English; 7.4% in the speech of secondary school teachers of disciplines other than English and 5.91% in the speech of medical doctors. These results are captured in the following bar chart.

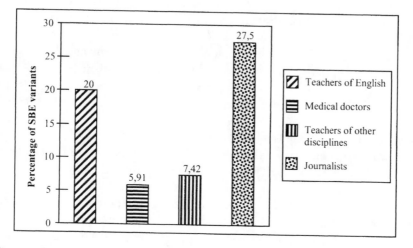

Figure 5: Occupationally-based correlation (effects of market pressure)

The chart shows that the scores of journalists and teachers of English considerably contrast with those of medical doctors and teachers of other disciplines. It can also be seen that journalists show a noticeable edge over secondary school teachers of English and teachers of disciplines other than English also show an edge over medical doctors. Generally, the scores of the different occupational groups reflect the extent to which they are influenced by market pressures to use the so-called standard forms of speech.

It should be noted that occupational status was studied in this work in terms of the concept of "market pressure" or in terms of the extent to which language-related occupations can influence the choice of "standard" forms of speech. Occupational status may not correlate considerably with linguistic variables in a New English context, such as Cameroon, if it does not match with level of education, as earlier argued in Chapter One. It should also be noted that the pattern of correlation that emerged in this work between linguistic variables and occupational status is still far below what has been observed in the Western world where informants are evaluated in terms of their variety of English. A more substantial correlation pattern is likely to emerge in Cameroon if speakers are evaluated in terms of their knowledge of standard CamE, which, unfortunately, is still to be determined.

4.5 Regionality-Based Correlation in Cameroon

The aim of investigating regional differences in speech was not to establish the dialect geography of different regions in Cameroon. The purpose was equally not to determine the extent to which a speaker's region influences his or her ability to approximate SBE variants, though this would be underscored in passing. The objective of studying urban and rural speech in this investigation, as pointed out in §2.7, was to determine the degree of phonological diversity in the speech of speakers who are permanently based in urban and rural areas. This objective was based on the assumption that urban speakers are exposed to people with different linguistic backgrounds and, as a result, their speech was expected to reflect the cosmopolitan setting of urban areas, unlike rural speakers who live a circumscribed type of life.

Through the analysis of the speech of 200 informants, evenly distributed according to whether they were resident in urban or rural areas, it was discovered that most of the linguistic variables studied did not show more diversity in the speech of urban speakers than in the speech of rural speakers, but those linguistic features which are neither those of mainstream CamE nor those of any native English were more frequent in the speech of urban female speakers than in the speech of those in the rural areas. This implies that the source of such linguistic features can either be attributed to female speakers' tendency to sound differently from their male counterparts or to the influence of a cosmopolitan setting which is characterized by a conglomeration of accents, because of the presence of people from different linguistic backgrounds. For example, the italicised grapheme of the word "cupboard" tended to yield three pronunciations, as earlier pointed out. No informant used the SBE variant [ə], irrespective of their region. The CamE variant [ɔ] was used by 95% of urban speakers and 100% of rural speakers. The variant which is of a particular interest here is [ʌ]. This variant, which is neither a SBE variant nor a CamE variant, did not occur at all in the speech of any rural speaker. The percentage of speakers who used this variant was 5% and all the speakers were urban female speakers.

As earlier pointed out, the main aim of studying urban and rural speech in this work was not to determine the extent to which urban and rural speakers approximated SBE variants. However, the percentage of SBE variants in the speech of the two categories of speakers was calculated, as was the case with the other extra-linguistic variables. It was revealed that the total average percentage of SBE in the speech of urban speakers was 5.15% and that of rural speakers was 4.31%. These scores show no substantial difference in the way the two categories of speakers used features of the variety of English that is promoted in Cameroon.

4.6 Ethnicity-Based Correlation

The wish to investigate the correlation between ethnicity and linguistic variables in this study was motivated by previous statements made about Bafut and Banso speakers of English, as earlier pointed out in §2.3. As concerns the Bafut tribe, it has, in fact, been established that the voiceless bilabial plosive [p] and the alveolar roll [r] (not included in the scope of this investigation) are very infrequent in the speech of speakers of English from this tribe. It has equally been established that the diphthong [əʊ] is not common in the speech of Banso speakers of English. The aim of restudying the speech of speakers of English from Bafut and Banso was to further investigate the extent to which the occurrence of [p] and [əʊ] in the speech of the speakers can be neutralized by educational attainment.

The analysis of the speech of 60 speakers per tribe who had undergone university education revealed a number of interesting findings, as shown in table 4n below.

Table 4n: Percentage of ethnicity-based linguistic variants in the speech of speakers with a university education

	Variants		Bafut	Banso	Bamileke	Bangwa	Bakweri
Items	SBE	CamE	%	%	%	%	%
post office	p[əʊ]st office		8.3	6.7	5	5	10
		p[o]st office	91.7	91.7	95	95	90
		p[u]st office	0	1.7	0	0	0
post office	[p]ost office		100	100	100	100	100
		[b]ost office	0	0	0	0	0

Interestingly, the sound [u], instead of SBE [əʊ] and mainstream CamE [o], which was previously associated with Banso speakers of English, was found only in the speech of a single Banso speaker with a university education. The mainstream CamE variant was used by 91.7% of speakers of English from this tribe and the SBE variant was used by 8.3% of the speakers. As concerns the voiced bilabial plosive [b] which has been said to characterize the speech of Bafut speakers of English at syllable-initial position, the analysis revealed that no speaker from Bafut with a university level of education used this feature.

The implication of these findings is that educational attainment can significantly neutralize mother tongue effects. It is therefore misleading to generalise, at least in the case of Cameroon, that speakers from a particular tribe display a certain linguistic tendency without making reference to the level of education of such speakers. This view is buttressed by the fact that the sounds [b] (for SBE [p] at word-initial or syllable-initial position) and [u] (for SBE [əʊ]) which have previously been associated with the Bafut and Banso tribes, respectively, tended to be lacking in the speech of speakers from these tribes who had attained a university level of education. In the case of Nigeria, for instance, the situation is very different; speakers from the major tribes (Hausa, Yoruba and Igbo) have very distinctive linguistic peculiarities which do not depend much on educational attainment.

4.7 The Correlation between Phonological Styles and Linguistic Variables

As pointed out in Chapter Three, the speech of the three categories of speakers selected according to level of education was evaluated in different phonological styles, which include, in descending order of formality, Minimal Pairs (MP), Word List Style (WLS), Sentence Reading Style (SRS), Passage Reading Style (PRS) and Casual Style (CS). The analysis showed that the speakers' ability to vary their speech according to the phonological styles depended much on the nature of the phonological variables and their level of education. As concerns the phonological variables evaluated, many of such variables did not show any substantial correlation with the different phonological styles (see Appendix 2). For instance, the SBE variant of the italicised grapheme of the word "happy" was lacking in the speech of most of the informants, irrespective of the phonological style under which the variable was evaluated. In spite of this lack of a substantial correlation, linguistic variables in Minimal Pairs yielded very high percentages of SBE realisations, as the following table shows.

Table 4o: The approximation of SBE features in Minimal Pairs

Items	Variants		Secondary school students	Undergraduate students	Postgraduate students
	SBE	CamE	%	%	%
foot	f[ʊ]t		8	25	34
		f[u]t	92	75	66
food	f[u:]d		11	29	33
		f[u]d	89	71	67
pull	p[ʊ]l		7	37	39
		p[u]l	93	63	61
pool	p[u:]l		13	40	52
		p[u]l	87	60	48
sit	s[ɪ]t		22	37	61
		s[i]t	78	63	39
seat	s[i:]t		14	51	62
		s[i]t	86	49	38
bit	b[ɪ]t		19	32	44
		b[i]t	81	68	56
beat	b[ɪ]t		11	36	55

Items	SBE	CamE	Secondary school students %	Undergraduate students %	Postgraduate students %
		b[i]t	89	64	45
cart	c[ɑ:]t		22	51	62
		c[a]t	78	49	38
cat	c[æ]t		0	0	2
		c[a]t	100	100	98
port	p[ɔ:]t		6	29	58
		p[ɔ]t	94	71	42
pot	p[ɒ]t		0	5	11
		p[ɔ]t	100	95	89
sot	s[ɒ]t		0	7	13
		s[ɔ]t	100	93	87
sort	s[ɔ:]t		21	42	44
		s[ɔ]t	79	58	56

The speakers' ability to show sensitivity to the different phonological styles also depended much on their level of education. As the table above also shows, the degree of approximation of SBE variants tends to be substantially higher in the speech of postgraduate students than in the speech of the other categories of students.

4.8 Mood-Based Correlation

It has been hypothesized in this study that the extent to which a speaker is speech-conscious also depends on whether he or she is in a negative mood (moods of fear and anger) or in a positive mood (mood of joy). Following the strategies described in Chapter Three, this hypothesis was systematically investigated. The analysis revealed different patterns of correlation, as was the case with the other extra-linguistic categories under study. There are a number of linguistic variables which showed a substantially correlation with the categories of mood (moods of anger, fear and joy) and there are some which were not considerably graded according to the moods of the speakers (see Appendix 8b for details).

In order to determine whether in the overall situation speakers used more SBE features in the mood of joy than in the moods of anger and fear, the total average percentage of SBE variants in the different moods was calculated. It was discovered that the total average percentage of SBE variants in the speech of the informants stood at 25% in the mood of anger, 22.3% in the mood of fear and 42.05% in the mood of joy, as the following bar chart illustrates.

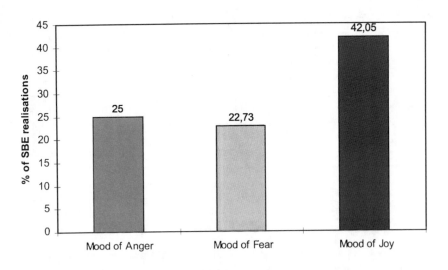

Figure 6: Percentages of SBE realisations in the moods of anger, fear and joy

The chart shows that there is no substantial difference between the informants' speech in the moods of anger and fear, in terms of speech consciousness. But the degree of speech-consciousness in the mood of joy is considerably higher than in the moods of anger and fear.

What therefore accounts for this correlation pattern between the categories of mood and linguistic variables? In the moods of anger and fear, the speakers are, predictably, in a negative mood. Being in such a mood, the tendency is to lack the psychological preparedness to be speech-conscious. But in the mood of joy, the speakers are in a positive mood, in which they tend to be more relaxed and consequently more prepared to be speech conscious. It is in a relaxed mood that the speakers can, in fact, set their speech-consciousness nerves at work. It should also be noted that this correlation pattern between linguistic variables and the different moods considered in the study could be more substantial if informants were evaluated in terms of their knowledge of educated CamE features.

Chapter Five
Conclusion
Summarizing and Situating the Findings within Current Sociolinguistic Thinking

5. Introduction

As pointed out in the General Introduction of this book, Inner Circle English norms continue to be the official goal in the ELT industry in Cameroon, in spite of the numerous studies carried out to show that features of such varieties of English are significantly lacking in the speech of Cameroonian users of English (see Chapter One for evidence from numerous studies on CamE). As a further attempt to investigate whether the goal to implant in Cameroon an Inner Circle English, such as SBE, has created any significant impact, CamE was studied in this work within the context of some social categories. The correlation patterns that emerge in this study between English linguistic variables and the social categories show the extent to which the patterns reported in the Western world prevail in a context with different sociolinguistic and cultural realities. The correlation patterns obtained in this study equally show whether attempts to implant SBE in Cameroon have yielded any fruits.

This chapter summarises and attempts to situate the findings of the study within the existing sociolinguistic knowledge. In order to do this, the highlights of the findings are succinctly recapitulated according to the different social categories under study and the sociolinguistic relevance or implication is underscored. In this attempt, it would be established whether the findings confirm or refute previous views.

5.1 Educationally-Based Correlation and the Sociolinguistic Relevance

In the previous chapter, it was established that the total average percentage of SBE features stood at 4.69% in the speech of secondary school students; 12.12% in the speech of undergraduate students and 17.85% in the speech of postgraduate students. These results imply that CamE features were dominant in the speech of postgraduate students, more dominant in the speech of undergraduate students and most dominant in the speech of secondary school students. In spite of this substantial correlation between level of education and English linguistic variables, it should be acknowledged that such results are far below what has been reported in Western English contexts. In such contexts, speakers are evaluated in terms of their knowledge of their mother tongue language, but most Cameroonians learn English after having acquired a good knowledge of one or more of the over 280 indigenous languages and Kamtok, an English-based Creole which has become a widely spoken lingua franca in Cameroon. This implies that the learning of English in a highly multilingual context, such as Cameroon, is not likely to yield the type of results expected in a mother tongue English environment, such as Britain and the United States.

The fact that the analysis showed a substantial correlation between SBE and level of education, but revealed a very low approximation of features of such a variety of English, suggests that a more interesting correlation pattern is likely to be obtained if Cameroonian speakers of English are evaluated in terms of their knowledge of educated features of their local variety of English. One of the arguments often advanced to discourage the promotion of CamE is that the variety is not yet standardized and only mother tongue varieties of English tend to guarantee educational and professional prospects. But it should be noted that the goal to target SBE features in Cameroon will hardly ever yield the expected results. Mainstream educated CamE features can be determined and promoted in the Cameroonian classroom, given that typical CamE has become the unavoidable companion of most Cameroonians and many of them tend to be proud of their variety of English (see Mbangwana 1987). Interestingly, in some Western institutions of higher learning, the recognition of the New Englishes as self-contained systems of communication has resulted in the inclusion of such varieties of English in the teaching and learning program. The fact that many people have won international awards to carry out research on some of the New Englishes further confirm that such varieties of English are no more seen as concoctions of mistakes, as was the case a few years ago.

We can therefore maintain that CamE needs to be standardized and promoted in the Cameroonian classroom. The fact that students with the highest level of education had a very low percentage of SBE features in their speech suggests that the teaching and promotion of this variety of English in Cameroon to the detriment of CamE is an unrealistic goal. In the same light, it is also unrealistic to evaluate Cameroonian speakers of English in terms of their knowledge of a variety of English that is psychologically and physically far remote from them. A more substantial correlation between level of education and English linguistic variables is likely to emerge if Cameroonian speakers of English are evaluated in terms of their local variety of English, which is significantly different from, say, SBE, as a result of the many twists and turns it has undergone because of the ecological, cultural and sociolinguistic realities of Cameroon.

5.2 Gender-Based Correlation in Cameroon and the Sociolinguistic Implications

Unlike the universal view that women tend to use more standard forms of speech, it is discovered in this study that the approximation of features of SBE (the variety of English officially associated with prestige) does not depend on whether one is a female or a male speaker. The investigation reveals that, instead of taking a remarkable lead in the approximation of features that are officially associated with prestige, women rather show "an edge" over men in the use of phonological features that are neither those of the local accent (CamE accent) nor those of any mother tongue English accent. For instance, the pronunciation *diversified* found in female speech is neither observable in mainstream CamE nor in SBE. The fact that women actually strive to produce such linguistic features is an indication that they wish to sound differently from their male counterparts, like women in other communities, but their effort does not enable them to approximate features of the variety of English that is associated with prestige by education authorities.

The gender-based correlation that emerges in this study has far-reaching sociolinguistic implications. First, the pattern suggests that in Cameroon the notions of *prestige* and *standard* do not neatly enjoy the same meaning, a situation similar to what is reported in studies conducted in the Middle East (see §2.2.2.3). While educational authorities highly prioritize SBE, some Cameroonians, especially pragmatists, rather scorn at those who strive to approximate it (Mbangwana 1987). The fact that those who strive to approximate SBE or any other mother tongue English are looked upon with contempt, rather than admiration, is an indication that the SBE accent or any other Western accent is not necessarily the prestige accent, at least, to a good number of Cameroonian speakers of English. In addition, many Cameroonians, including female speakers, do not have a good mastery of this variety of English and any ambition to approximate its features is likely to be a futile one. As concerns the option of targeting CamE features in order to enjoy the prestige that women in other societies enjoy for using standard forms of speech, it should be noted that there are many polemics involved in such an option. In spite of pragmatists' positive attitude towards CamE, purists argue that its features are unintelligible to an international audience and, consequently, do not give its speakers access to international employment opportunities. Given such a situation, female speakers in Cameroon are caught up in a type of dilemma. Should they use CamE features and be accused by purists of speaking substandard English? Or should they target SBE features, even when they have no mastery of such a variety of English? In the case of those who have a good mastery of SBE, should they use features of such a variety of English and be "ridiculed rather than being admired" (Mbangwana 1987)? These questions show the dilemma in which female speakers find themselves in a context such as Cameroon where there is no unanimity on what constitutes prestige English linguistic features. If CamE is eventually standardised and purists develop a positive attitude towards it, stigma-free educated CamE features will acquire the type of prestige associated with standard linguistic features in mother tongue English contexts. In this case, a gender-based linguistic investigation in Cameroon that evaluates speakers in terms of their approximation of standard CamE features is likely to obtain results similar to what has been reported in the numerous studies conducted in the Western world.

5.3 Age-Based Correlation and the Sociolinguistic Implications

The most striking age-based correlation that emerges in this study, as underscored in Chapter Four, shows a situation where there is a remarkable increase in the use of SBE features as one climbs the age ladder. The percentage of SBE features stood at 4% in the speech of speakers between the ages of 12 and 19; 6.68% in the speech of speakers between 20 and 30; 10.7% in the speech of speakers between 31 and 49 and 8.68% in the speech of speakers above 49. In spite of the fact that the score of speakers between 31 and 49 years is higher than that of speakers above 49, the general pattern shows that SBE features were more frequent in the speech of older speakers than in the speech of younger ones. The pattern that emerges in this work is similar to the one reported in Chambers (1995), but the difference between the pattern that emerges in this study and the one reported in Chambers (ibid.) lies at the level of the reasons that account for the two patterns. Chambers (1995) sees the use of non-standard forms of speech by the younger generation as a conscious effort to violate linguistic norms in order to create a linguistic identity. In fact, he maintains that the infrequency of standard linguistic features in the speech of the younger generation is a consequence of their 'rebellious' tendency to reverse the highly prized institutions of the older generation.

Chambers' explanation is likely to account for an age-based correlation that involves linguistic levels other than phonology, irrespective of the community in which the investigation is carried out. At the lexico-syntactic level, the tendency for the youth to establish a specialised vocabulary and special syntactic forms is quite observable even in Cameroon, as Chambers (ibid.) postulates, but the phenomenon is not common at the level of phonology, the focus of this study. In effect, what emerges in this study as age differences in speech is more of a consequence of differences in level of education. Younger speakers, logically, cannot be striving to create a linguistic identity at the level of phonology when they, like most Cameroonians, are far distant from the SBE accent. In reality, the level of education of young speakers has not exposed them to SBE features to the same degree as older speakers whose level of education tends to be higher (than that of younger speakers). This implies that in investigating age-based linguistic correlation in a New English context, such as Cameroon, one may run the risk of considering differences in level of education to be differences in age. The tendency to run such a risk is higher in New English contexts because education is the only itinerary though which people are exposed to the Inner Circle English accent and older speakers have a higher likelihood, through schooling, to be exposed to such features than younger speakers. But in Inner Circle English contexts, the mother tongue accent is quite 'rampant' and, in this case, education cannot be the principal means to expose speakers to such an accent.

The observation that younger English speakers in Cameroon do not seek to establish a linguistic identity at the level of English pronunciation has a sociolinguistic implication. In fact, it suggests that the tendency to create a linguistic identity depends much on the speakers' knowledge of the language. The domain of English phonology happens to be the most problematic linguistic level to speakers of the New Englishes who still depend on mother tongue English norms. This therefore implies that the relative lack of SBE features in the speech of the younger speakers in this study cannot be seen as a conscious effort to violate linguistic norms in order to create an identity, given that they do not have a good mastery of SBE accent.

5.4 Occupationally-Based Correlation and the Sociolinguistic Relevance

As underscored in §4.4, occupation has been studied in this work in terms of "market pressures" or in terms of the extent to which a speaker's profession influences him or her to choose linguistic variants of the variety of English that is officially targeted in Cameroon. The analysis of the data shows that the total average percentage of SBE realisations stood at 27.5% in the speech of journalists; 20% in the speech of teachers of English; 7.42% in the speech of teachers of disciplines other than English and 5.91% in the speech of medical doctors. This pattern of correlation, substantially graded according to market pressures, is similar to the pattern speculated in Sankoff et al. (1989). As pointed out in Chapter Two, Sankoff et al. (ibid.) have actually established that society expects certain professionals to use more standard forms of speech than others. In the context of this work, it can be noticed that the scores of journalists and that of teachers of English are considerably higher than those of teachers of other disciplines and medical doctors. The score of journalists, in turn, is higher than that of teachers of English; and that of teachers of other disciplines also tends to be higher than that of medical doctors. One would have expected no striking difference between the scores of journalists and that of teachers of English, given that the pressure on them is almost of the same degree. The fact that medical doctors used the lowest percentage of SBE features and journalists used the highest percentage of such features confirms the hypothesis that among the four categories of speakers, medical doctors are under the least pressure to use "standard" forms of speech and journalists are under the highest pressure to use such features.

It should however be pointed out that the degree of approximation of SBE features in the speech of the four groups of speakers remains far below what is likely to be the outcome if the same categories of speakers were evaluated, say, in Britain. In a context such as Cameroon, SBE features remain highly inaccessible even to speakers like journalists and teachers of English who have the highest pressure to use standard forms of speech. It is certainly surprising that the total average percentage of SBE features in the speech of journalists is as low as 27.5%. The effects of "market pressure" are therefore likely to be more glaring in a study that evaluates speakers of different professions according to their knowledge of educated CamE phonological features.

5.5 Regionality-Based Correlation and the Sociolinguistic Relevance

It was reported in §4.5 that those phonological variants identified in female speakers' speech were also found to be more frequent in the speech of urban female speakers than in the speech of rural female speakers. Such variants can either be associated with women's tendency to create unique linguistic variants or they may simply reflect the influence of a cosmopolitan setting where speakers with different linguistic backgrounds interact together.   Since the variants were found only in the speech of urban female informants, one can maintain that there is a higher likelihood for linguistic diversity to occur in the speech of urban speakers than in the speech of rural speakers. Rural speakers, in fact, have a limited exposure to people with different English accents, but urban speakers interact with people from a wide range of linguistic backgrounds and linguistic influences are likely to take place.

In spite of the fact that this linguistic diversity does not emerge very glaringly in this investigation, as originally predicted, a pronunciation such as "hard w[ɛ]king", for mainstream CamE "hard w[ɔ]king", is an aspect of other African Englishes. For instance, such a variant is obtainable in Ghanaian English, Tanzanian English and Southern African Black English. It should also be noted that those pronunciation features which are associated with urban female speakers in this work may simply be tendencies of hypercorrection. This implies that a further investigation is needed to determine the exact sources of such variants.

5.6 Ethnicity-Based Correlation and the Sociolinguistic Implications

The aim of studying ethnicity in this work, as earlier pointed out in §2.6 and §4.6, was not to evaluate the impact of mother-tongue languages of selected tribes on the English language, as is the case in Jibril (1982) and related studies. The aim was to further evaluate the extent to which level of education is likely to influence the speech of Bafut and Banso speakers of English in the pronunciation of [p] at syllable-initial position and [əʊ] respectively. The inclusion of such tribes as Bamileke, Bangwa and Bakweri was an attempt to compare the speech of speakers from these tribes to that of Bafut and Banso speakers of English in the pronunciation of the above sounds.

As pointed out in the previous chapter, the analysis of the data shows that the sound [b], which has been reported in previous studies (e.g. Mushing 1989) to be the substitute of [p] in the speech of some Bafut speakers of English, was not found in the speech of any informant from this tribe with a university education. The sound was not equally found in the speech of any informant from the other tribes. It was also discovered that only 1.7% of speakers from Banso with a university level of education replaced the diphthong [əʊ] with [u].

The implication of these findings is that educational attainment can significantly neutralize mother-tongue-effects. This view is supported by the fact that speakers with a university education from the tribes which have been associated with certain sounds end up lacking those sounds in their speech. This further suggests that it may be misleading to claim that speakers from a particular tribe in Cameroon display a certain linguistic tendency without making reference to the level of education of such speakers. In the case of Nigeria, as pointed out in §4.6, the situation is not in any way comparable to what is obtained in Cameroon. The major ethnic groups in Nigeria display systematic and stable linguistic peculiarities which do not depend much on the level of education of the speakers (see Jibril 1982).

5.7 Phonological Style-Based Correlation and the Sociolinguistic Relevance

As discussed in the previous chapter, the ability of the informants of this study to vary their speech according to the phonological styles depended much on the nature of the phonological variables evaluated and the level of education of the speakers. As concerns the phonological variables evaluated, many of such variables did not show any predictable correlation with the different phonological styles, but linguistic variables in Minimal Pairs yielded very high percentages of SBE realisations. As concerns the level of education of the speakers, the degree of approximation of SBE features was relatively higher in the speech of postgraduate students, especially in Minimal Pairs, than in the speech of undergraduate students and secondary school students.

If it is concluded that the informants' ability to show sensitivity to the different phonological styles depend much on the nature of the linguistic variables evaluated and on their level of education, what are the sociolinguistic implications? First, it implies that those sounds that do not fall within the sound system of CamE (e.g. [æ]) posed more difficulties to the informants than those that are familiar to them. Second, if the informants were evaluated according to their knowledge of educated features of CamE, the variety of English that is in harmony with their souls, they would show more sensitivity to the expectations of the different phonological styles, like speakers of English in places such as the UK and the US.

5.8 Mood-Based Correlation and the Sociolinguistic Relevance

The discussion underscored in §4.8 clearly shows that a speaker's mood or the state of his or her feelings at a particular time has a remarkable influence on his or her speech. This pattern is explained by the fact that, in a positive mood (mood of joy), the speakers are more likely to be speech-conscious than when they are in a negative mood (moods of fear and anger). The possible sociolinguistic implication is that a new dimension of studying speech variation is being postulated and claimed in this investigation and this implies that, in addition to traditional sociolinguistic categories (gender, age, etc.), the mood of a speaker can also yield significant linguistic variability.

But it should be noted that a more predictable and substantial correlation between linguistic variables and the mood of a speaker is likely to emerge if speakers are evaluated according to their ability to use a variety of English that is in harmony with their souls. In spite of all the efforts made to implant SBE in Cameroon, many Cameroonians remain real strangers to it. If CamE is eventually standardized and informants are evaluated in terms of their approximation of standard CamE features, there is a high likelihood that a more predictable pattern of correlation between linguistic variables and the speakers' mood will emerge.

5.9 General Sociolinguistic Implications

If ELT goals in Cameroon continue to target Western models of English, it implies that educational authorities in Cameroon are assuming a universal standard of English that should be the destination of every learner and speaker of English, irrespective of the context in which they find themselves. Interestingly, most of the correlation patterns that emerge in this work show a marked difference from what has been reported in studies conducted in the Western world, especially in terms of the degree of approximation of "standard" English features. None of the social categories studied enabled speakers to approximate "standard" English linguistic features to the same degree as those in mother tongue English contexts, such as the UK and the US. What are therefore the general sociolinguistic implications for the fact that speakers drawn from different educational strata, age groups, occupational groups and so on, generally, showed very little knowledge of features of the variety of English that is promoted in Cameroon?

The first sociolinguistic implication is that Standard (?) CamE is a better choice than SBE for Cameroonian speakers of English in general and Cameroonian learners in particular. If a norm is elected for CamE at all linguistic levels, studies of this nature will rather rely on CamE as the reference variety of English rather than on a variety of English, such as SBE, whose features are challenging even to those who claim to be teaching it. If Standard CamE is determined and promoted on the Cameroonian landscape and research subjects are evaluated in terms of their knowledge of the standard features of their local variety of English, there is no doubt that studies on correlation will yield the type of significant patterns reported in the Western world. The absence of a consensus on what constitutes prestige English linguistic features in Cameroon puts many speakers in a state of dilemma. It is for this reason that speakers drawn from certain social categories (e.g. gender) end up producing linguistic variants that reflect this dilemma.

It should be noted that in spite of efforts to implant Western models of English in Cameroon, speakers who attempt to speak with an Inner Circle accent are seen as objects of ridicule rather than being admired (Mbangwana 1987). Yet, those who speak typical Cameroon English are seen as speakers of substandard English. In order for the standardization process of CamE to become a reality, educational authorities need to develop a more positive attitude towards it and should make clear-cut statements that recognize CamE as a self-contained system of communication that carries the Cameroonian identity and culture.

The second implication has to do with whether it is even necessary and realistic to implant, say, SBE in a context, such as Cameroon, which has sociocultural and sociolinguistic realities different from those of Western countries. In a context where almost everybody is a polyglot, can a Western model of English be successfully learned without heavy linguistic interference from the numerous languages spoken in Cameroon? How many language or linguistic departments in secondary schools and universities in Cameroon have language laboratories for the effective teaching of Western models of English? In some institutions, it is conspicuously inscribed "language laboratory" on certain doors, yet there is no single instrument in these rooms which has been preserved for the effective teaching of the language. How many British and American teachers of English have been recruited by the government to teach such models of English in Cameroon? Instead of wasting time and energy targeting Western models of English in Cameroon, the necessary resources can be put together to accelerate the process of standardization of Cameroon English, which carries the minds and hearts of most Cameroonians.

The study of CamE from the context of the different social categories investigated is a further attempt to tell a well-known story from a different perspective. From the time of Masanga (1983) through Mbangwana (1987), Kouega (1991), Bobda (1994) to Atechi (1996), many efforts have been made to testify, through description, that CamE is significantly different from Western models of English. This work studies the difference between CamE and a Western model of English in terms of the difference between Western world correlation patterns and those that prevail in a New English context, such as Cameroon, though the investigation had a number of different goals other than just comparing patterns. In spite of the fact that the approximation of SBE features was substantially graded according to the categories of some of the sociolinguistic variables under study (e.g. level of education and occupational status), the degree of approximation of features of the variety of English that is promoted in Cameroon was very low, compared to what is reported in studies conducted in the Western world. In a number of cases, no considerable correlation emerged between SBE and the social categories. For instance, male and female speakers showed no considerable difference in the way they approximated the SBE variants of the linguistic variables investigated. In the study of the correlation between the speakers' moods and linguistic variables, the use of SBE features was substantially graded according to the speakers' moods, but the correlation pattern could be more striking if the informants were evaluated in terms of their knowledge of standard features of CamE, if it was already a standardized variety. At this point in time, there is still an absence of a consensus on what constitutes the norm within the context of CamE and what should be castigated as stigmatized forms.

Appendices

Appendix 1a: Background information

Sex::...
Level of education: ....
Ethnic group: ....
Age: ....
Occupation:...
Permanent place of residence:..
Length of time in the permanent place of resident:: ....

Appendix 1b: Exercises involving the phonological variables under investigation

I- Read the following pairs of words aloud (Minima Pairs).

foot	food		cat	cart
pull	pool		pot	port
sit	seat		sot	sort
bit	beat			

II. Please, also read the following words aloud (Word List Style).

Cupboard, hardworking, drugs, Mary, chairs, period, mere, village, singing, recent, create aren't, laudable, satan, success, legal, penal, castle, pestle, bosom, tour, Joan, said, liquid, of, bad, bag, dog, consumption, nursery, basic, conserve, muscle, increasing, president, Joseph, visitor, position, reside, clumsy, opposite, maximum, flexible, exodus, fuel, population, journalist, typist, first, post office, happy, sad, interesting, commented, preparatory, ancestors, explanatory, challenging, authoritative, success, ceremony, advice, category, favouritism, colleague, journalism, purchase, nepotism, biased, referee, combat, jubilee, embarrass, Vivian, impossible, Eunice, irrelevant, Helen, illogical, insurance, however, classified, criticised, satisfied, diversified.

III. Read the following sentences aloud:

1) It is interesting to remark that *Vivian* courageously challenged our ancestors.
2) Professor Maximum qualified our *referees* as incompetent adventurers.
3) Vivian, my colleague, seriously appreciated *Helen*'s advice to the population.

4) The month of December has been programmed for the *ceremony*, marking the Silver *Jubilee* of the president.

5) The journalists felt that it is impossible for our *authoritative* leaders to believe that *nepotism* necessarily brings about bad leadership.

6) The jury's decision created a certain degree of imbalance in the president of the committee who commented that the verdict was characterised by bias and *favouritism* .

7) The typist refused to visit the post office because *Eunice* failed to provide an explanatory reason for the visit .

8) *Journalism* does not have only a single *category* of broadcasters.

IV. Read the following speech, assuming that your audience is made up of very important personalities, some of which include Ministers, Directors and other important guests:

Your Excellency, the Minister of Territorial Administration,
Your Excellency, the Minister of Women's Affairs,
Distinguished guests,
Ladies and Gentlemen:
It is a singular pleasure to welcome you to this important occasion. In fact, I find it quite *interesting* to talk to you today in my new capacity as the Mayor of this town. Many of our visitors in this town have testified that I am certainly going to be a very serious administrative officer. In fact, Mrs Eunice and Dr Vivian, my *colleagues* from Korea, *commented* during their last visit to Cameroon that I can be *classified* among the best leaders. Their observation was based on the fact that I told that my government is not characterised by nepotism and favouritism. They also *classified* Cameroon as a country with a *diversified*_culture.

This ceremony is also a good opportunity for us to point out that our journalists have a task which is quite *challenging*. They need to give *advice* to the never-*satisfied*-illiterates who have often *criticised* the government without any genuine *explanatory* reason. In fact, it is *illogical* and even embarrassing for people to be *biased* in their thinking to the extent of assuming that we are not making efforts to *combat* economic crisis. It is also *irrelevant* for people to think that the only way to combat economic crisis is to *purchase* and consume our locally produced goods.

Distinguished guests, I will use this opportunity to remark that the Senior Divisional Officer has, *however*, taken the decision to maximise his efforts in providing the best services to the population during his term of office. Your advice and that of our *ancestors* will be of great help to him.

Distinguished guests, Ladies and Gentlemen, the president of this country promised to use his position to ensure an effective management of our natural resources and to create an *insurance* scheme for the population. He also promised to create ten nursery schools by the month of December. We should all be prepared to appreciate his laudable efforts to raise our standard of living. We should also note that the *success* of the president's plan of action depends on our maximum co-operation. It was *impossible* for him to take part in this ceremony because of his involvement in a preparatory meeting to welcome the African scientists to Cameroon.

Distinguished guests, Ladies and Gentlemen, I wish you a happy stay here and a successful journey to your various homes. Thank you very much for listening to my speech.

Appendix 2: Percentages of SBE and CamE variants in the speech of the different categories of students in different phonological styles

Minimal Pairs

Items	Variants		Secondary school students (S)	Undergraduate students (U)	Postgraduate students (P)
	SBE	CamE	%	%	%
foot	f[ʊ]t		8	25	34
		f[u]t	92	75	66
food	f[u:]d		11	29	33
		f[u]d	89	71	67
pull	p[ʊ]l		7	37	39
		p[u]l	93	63	61
pool	p[u:]l		13	40	52
		p[u]l	87	60	48
sit	s[ɪ]t		22	37	61
		s[i]t	78	63	39
seat	s[i:]t		14	51	62
		s[i]t	86	49	38
bit	b[ɪ]t		19	32	44
		b[i]t	81	68	56
beat	b[ɪ]t		11	36	55
		b[i]t	89	64	45
cart	c[ɑ:]t		22	51	62
		c[a]t	78	49	38
cat	c[æ]t		0	0	2
		c[a]t	100	100	98
port	p[ɔ:]t		6	29	58
		p[ɔ]t	94	71	42
pot	p[ɒ]t		0	5	11
		p[ɔ]t	100	95	89
sot	s[ɒ]t		0	7	13

Word List Style

	Variants		S %	U %	P %
cupboard	cupb[ə]d		0	2	7

		cupb[ɔ]d	99	95	90
		cupb[e]d	1	3	3
hardworking	hardw[ə:]king		0	11	17
		hardw[ɔ]king	98	69	54
		hardw[e]king	2	16	26
		hardw[ə]king	0	4	13
drugs	dr[ʌ]gs		0	3	11
		dr[ɔ]gs	100	97	89
Mary	M[ɛə]ry		1	4	4
		M[ei]ry	5	13	22
		M[e]ry	94	83	74
chairs	ch[ɛə]s		0	2	9
		ch[iə]s	92	90	82
		ch[iɛ]s	3	1	5
		ch[ie]s	5	7	4
period	p[ɪə]riod		0	0	1
		p[i]riod	100	100	99
		p[ie]riod	0	0	0
mere	m[ɪə]		0	3	5
		m[ɛ]	81	82	80
		m[ei]	19	15	15
village	vill[i]ge		0	0	4
		vill[e]ge	100	100	96
satan	s[eɪ]tan		1	16	28
		s[a]tan	99	80	59
		s[ɛ]tan	0	4	13
laudable	l[ɔ:]dable		0	3	11
		l[au]dable	100	97	89
aren't	[ɑ:nt]		0	6	6
		[arənt]	85	82	75
		[arent]	15	12	19
create	cr[i:ie]te		1	7	12
		cr[eɪ]te	78	89	88
		cr[ɛ]te	21	4	0
Joan	J[əʊ]n		0	22	31
		J[ɔa]n	100	78	69
said	sai[d]		0	0	2
		sai[t]	100	100	98
liquid	liqui[d]		5	12	18
		liqui[t]	95	88	82
of	o[v]		0	0	0
		o[f]	100	100	100
bad	ba[d]		7	29	42
		ba[t]	93	71	58
bag	ba[g]		2	11	13
		ba[k]	98	89	87

dog	do[g]		2	5	5
		do[k]	98	95	95
basic	ba[s]ic		12	16	19
		ba[z]ic	88	84	81
recaent	r[i:]cent		5	11	24
		r[e]cent	82	71	65
		r[ɛ]cent	13	18	11
singing	si[ŋiŋ]		0	3	29
		si[ngin]	100	97	71
legal	l[i:]gal		2	17	31
		l[e]gal	98	83	69
penal	p[i:]nal		2	17	31
		p[e]nal	91	83	69
		p[ɛ]nal	7	3	9
castle	cas[ø]le		4	44	62
		cas[t]le	96	56	38
pestle	pes[ø]le		11	49	72
		pes[t]le	89	51	28
bosom	b[ʊ]som		0	0	6
		b[ɔ]som	100	100	94
tour	t[ʊə]		0	4	7
		t[ɔ]	100	96	93
visitor	vi[z]itor		0	1	4
		vi[s]itor	100	99	96
position	po[z]ition		0	1	2
		po[s]ition	100	99	98
reside	re[z]ide		0	0	2
		re[s]ide	100	100	98
clumsy	clum[z]y		1	3	4
		clum[s]y	99	97	96
opposite	opp[z]ite		1	5	7
		opp[s]ite	99	95	93
maximum	ma[ks]imum		0	0	4
		ma[gz]imum	17	11	12
		ma[kz]imum	83	89	84
flexible	fle[ks]ible		0	5	5
		fle[gz]ible	24	7	8
		fle[kz]ible	76	88	87
consumption	con[s]umption		0	5	5
		con[z]umption	100	95	95
nursery	nur[s]ery		0	2	4
		nur[z]ery	100	98	96
December	De[s]ember		0	7	13
		De[z]ember	100	93	87
conserve	con[s]erve		0	0	3
		con[z]erve	100	100	97

muscle	mu[s]cle		0	4	5
	mu[z]cle		100	96	95
increasing	increa[s]ing		2	7	9
	increa[z]ing		98	93	91
president	pre[z]ident		0	1	5
	pre[s]ident		100	99	95
Joseph	Jo[z]eph		0	0	0
	Jo[s]eph		100	100	100
exodus	e[ks]odus		0	1	3
	e[gz]odus		18	15	7
	e[kz]odus		82	84	90
fuel	f[ju]el		3	8	13
	f[u]el		97	92	87
population	pop[ju]lation		1	4	11
	pop[u]lation		99	96	89
journalist	journalis[t]		13	37	44
	journalis[ø]		87	63	56
typist	typsi[t]		15	39	47
	typsi[ø]		85	61	53
first	firs[t]		8	33	39
	firs[ø]		92	67	61
post office	pos[t] office		4	22	43
	pos[ø] office		96	78	57
post office	p[əu]st office		2	4	13
	p[o]st office		98	96	87
	p[u]st office		0	0	0
post office	[p]ost office		100	100	100
	[b]ost office		0	0	0

CS, PRS and WLS

	Variants		CS			PRS			WLS		
			S	U	P	S	U	P	S	U	P
Lexical items	SBE	CamE	%	%	%	%	%	%	%	%	%
success	s[ə]ccess		0	2	1	0	4	8	0	7	11
		s[ɔ]ccess	100	98	99	100	96	92	100	93	89
happy	h[æ]ppy		0	0	0	0	0	2	0	0	1
		h[a]ppy	100	100	100	100	100	98	100	100	99
sad	sa[d]		7	9	19				7	13	19
		sa[t]	93	91	81				93	87	81

commen-ted	'commen-ted				0	0	0	0	0	1
	com'men-ted				100	100	100	100	100	99
combat	'combat				0	7	24	0	13	24
	com'bat				100	93	76	100	87	76
colleague	'colleague				0	0	5	0	2	7
	col'league				100	100	95	100	98	93
challen-ging	'challen-ging				0	0	1	0	0	3
	chal'len-ging				100	100	99	100	100	97
ancestors	'ancestors				0	3	11	1	6	25
	an'cestors				100	97	89	99	94	75
purchase	'purchase				0	1	4	0	1	5
	pur'chase				100	99	96	100	99	95
success	suc'cess	0	0	1	0	2	5	0	2	11
	'success	100	100	99	100	98	95	100	98	89
advice	ad'vice				2	11	13	4	9	13
	'advice				98	89	87	96	91	87
biased	'biased				0	0	5	0	0	9
	bi'ased				100	100	95	100	100	91
interesting	'interes-ting				2	4	11	2	7	13
	inte'res-ting				98	96	89	98	93	87
embarrass	em'bar-rass				0	0	4	0	0	4
	embar'-rass				100	100	96	100	100	96
however	how'ever				0	0	1	0	0	1
	'however				100	100	99	100	100	99
insurance	in'surance				0	1	1	0	1	2
	'insurance				100	99	99	100	99	98
illogical	il'logical				0	0	0	0	0	1
	'illogical				100	100	100	100	100	99
irrelevant	ir'relevant				0	0	1	0	0	2
	'irrelevant				100	100	99	100	100	98
impossible	im'pos-sible				0	2	3	0	2	4
	'impos-sible				100	98	97	100	98	96
classified	'classified				0	2	5	0	4	6
	classi'fied				100	98	95	100	96	94
satisfied	'satisfied				0	3	4	0	3	5
	satis'fied				100	97	96	100	97	95
criticised	'criticised				0	1	5	0	3	11
	criti'cised				100	99	95	100	97	89
diversified	di'versified				0	0	0	0	0	0
	Diversi-'fied				100	100	93	100	99	88
	'diversified				0	0	7	0	1	12
prepara-tory	pre'para-tory				0	0	1	0	0	1

		prepa'ratory				100	100	99	100	100	99
explana-tory	ex'plana-tory					0	0	1	0	0	1
		expla'natory				100	100	99	100	100	99

SRS and WLS

	Variants		SRS			WLS		
			S	U	P	S	U	P
Lexical items	SBE	CamE	%	%	%	%	%	%
authoritative	au'thoritative		0	0	1	0	0	1
		authori'tative	100	100	99	100	100	99
ceremony	'ceremony		0	5	11	0	8	14
		ce'remony	100	95	89	100	92	86
category	'category		0	3	9	0	4	11
		ca'tegory	100	97	81	100	96	89
favouritism	'favouritism		0	0	2	0	1	3
		favou'ritism	100	100	98	100	99	97
journalism	'journalism		0	2	14	0	4	16
		jour'nalism	100	98	86	100	96	84
nepotism	'nepotism		0	0	5	0	1	7
		ne'potism	100	100	95	100	99	93
referee	refe'ree		69	37	31	67	38	33
		'referee	31	63	69	33	62	67
jubilee	'jubilee		0	0	0	0	0	0
		jubi'lee	100	100	100	100	100	100
Vivian	'Vivian		3	32	60	2	35	33
		Vi'vian	97	68	40	98	65	67
Eunice	'Eunice		5	43	63	5	49	
		Eu'nice	95	57	37	95	51	41
Helen	'Helen		2	58	64	3	58	66
		He'len	98	42	36	97	42	34

Appendix 3: Percentages of SBE and CamE variants in the speech of male and female speakers
Phonological style: WLS
Total number of informants: 302
Number of informants per category: 151

items	Variants SBE	CamE	Men %	Women %
cupboard	cupb[ə]d		1.98	1.3
		cupb[ɔ]d	98	94
		cupb[ʌ]d	0	4.6
hardworking	hardw[ɔː]king		3.3	5.29
		hardw[ɔ]king	91.39	80.13
		hardweking	4.6	12.5
		hardw[ə]king	0.7	1.98
drugs	dr[ʌ]gs		1.98	1.98
		dr[ɔ]gs	98	98
Mary	M[ɛə]ry		1.3	0.7
		M[ei]ry	3.3	7.3
		M[e]ry	95.4	92
chairs	ch[ɛə]s		1.3	1.3
		ch[iə]s	96	80.1
		ch[iɛ]s	1.98	8.6
		ch[ie]s	0.7	9.9
period	p[iə]riod		0.7	0
		p[i]riod	99.3	97.4
		p[ie]riod	0	2.6
mere	m[ɪə]		1.98	0.7
		m[ɛ]	76.1	69.5
		m[ei]	21.9	29.8
village	vill[i]ge		0	0
		vill[e]ge	100	100
satan	s[eɪ]tan		5.29	5.96
		s[a]tan	91.39	82.12
		s[ɛ]tan	3.3	11.9
laudable	l[ɔː]dable		1.98	1.3
		l[au]dable	98	98.7
aren't	[aːnt]		0.7	5.29
		[arənt]	7.3	13.24
		[arent]	92	88
create	cr[iːeɪ]te		3.3	0.7
		cr[e]te	85.4	88
		cr[ɛ]te	11.2	11.2
recent	r[iː]cent		3.3	4.6
		r[e]cent	72.8	64.2
		r[ɛ]cent	23.8	31.1

singing	si[ŋiŋ]		0.7	1.9
		si[ngin]	99.3	98
legal	l[i:]gal		3.97	7.3
		l[e]gal	96	93.4
penal	p[i:]nal		3.3	4.6
		p[e]nal	84.8	81.4
		p[ɛ]nal	11.9	13.9
castle	cas[ø]le		24.5	25.82
		cas[t]le	75.49	74.17
pestle	pes[ø]le		24.5	21.85
		pes[t]le	75.49	78.14
bosom	b[ʊ]som		1.3	0
		b[ɔ]som	98.7	100
tour	t[ʊə]		1.98	0.7
		t[ɔ]	98	99.3
Joan	J[əʊ]n		6.6	7.3
		J[ɔa]n	93.3	92.7
said	sai[d]		0.7	1.3
		sai[t]	99.3	98.7
liquid	liqui[d]		7.94	4.6
		liqui[t]	92	95.4
of	o[v]		0	0
		o[f]	100	100
bad	ba[d]		9.93	7.94
		ba[t]	90	92
bag	ba[g]		5.96	3.97
		ba[k]	94	96.02
dog	do[g]		1.98	2.64
		do[k]	98	97.35
position	po[z]ition		1.3	0
		po[s]ition	98	100
basic	ba[s]ic		5.3	5.96
		ba[z]ic	94.7	94
reside	re[z]ide		0	1.3
		re[s]ide	100	98.6
clumbsy	clum[z]y		0.7	1.3
		clum[s]y	99.3	98.7
opposite	oppo[z]ite		1.3	1.98
		oppo[s]ite	98.7	98.02
maximum	ma[ks]imum		0	0.7
		ma[gz]imum	75.49	60.26
		ma[kz]imum	23.8	39
flexible	fle[ks]ible		0	3.3
		fle[gz]ible	70.1	55.6
		fle[kz]ible	29.8	7.9
consumption	con[s]umption		0.7	2.6

		con[z]umption	99.3	97.4
nursery	nur[s]ery		1.3	0
		nur[z]ery	98.7	100
December	De[s]ember		4.6	0.7
		De[z]ember	95.4	99.3
conserve	con[s]erve		0	0
		con[z]erve	100	100
muscle	mu[s]cle		2.6	0.7
		mu[z]cle	97.4	99.3
increasing	increa[s]ing		1.3	2.6
		increa[z]ing	98.7	97.4
president	pre[z]ident		0.7	0
		pre[s]ident	99.3	100
joseph	Jo[z]eph		0	0
		Jo[s]eph	100	100
exodus	e[ks]odus		0.7	0
		e[gz]odus	52.3	47.7
		e[kz]odus	47	52.3
fuel	f[jʊ]el		1.32	4.6
		f[u]el	98.7	95.4
population	pop[jʊ]lation		1.32	1.32
		pop[u]lation	98.7	98.7
journalist	journalis[t]		15.23	10.60
		journalis[ø]	84.77	89.4
typist	typis[t]		18.5	10.60
		typis[ø]	81.4	89.4
first	firs[t]		13.25	11.26
		firs[ø]	86.75	99.74
post office	pos[t] office		7.28	8.61
		pos[ø] office	92.72	91.39
post office	p[əʊ]st office		1.98	1.32
		p[o]st office	98.01	98.7
		p[u]st office	0	0
	[p]ost office		100	100
		[b]ost office	0	0
success	s[ə]ccess		3.97	0.7
		s[ɔ]ccess	96	99.3
happy	h[æ]ppy		0	0.7
		h[a]ppy	100	99.3
sad	sa[d]		4.6	4.6
		sa[t]	95.4	95.4
biased	'biased		0	0.7
		bi'ased	100	99.3
interesting	'interesting		2.65	2.65
		inte'resting	97.4	97.4
embarrass	em'barrass		0	0

		embar'rass	100	100
however	how'ever		0	0
		'however	100	100
insurance	in'surance		0.7	0
		'insurance	99.3	100
illogical	il'logical		0.7	0
		'illogical	99.3	100
irrelevant	ir'relevant		0	0
		'irrelevant	100	100
impossible	im'possible		0.7	1.3
		'impossible	99.3	98.7
commented	'commented		0	0
		com'mented	100	100
combat	'combat		4.6	5.3
		com'bat	95.4	94.7
colleague	'colleague		0	1.98
		col'league	100	98
challenging	'challenging		0	0.7
		chal'lenging	100	99.3
ancestors	'ancestors		2.6	1.3
		an'cestors	97.4	98.7
purchase	'purchase		1.32	0
		pur'chase	98.7	100
success	suc'cess		1.3	0
		'success	98.7	100
advice	ad'vice		3.97	1.98
		'advice	98	98
classified	'classified		1.3	1.98
		classi'fied	98.7	98
satisfied	'satisfied		0.7	1.3
		satis'fied	99.3	98.7
criticised	'criticised		0.7	1.3
		criti'cised	99.3	98.7
diversified	di'versified		0	0
		diversi'fied	100	92.7
		'diversified	0	7.3
preparatory	pre'paratory		0.7	0
		prepa'ratory	99.3	100
explanatory	ex'planatory		0.7	0
		expla'natory	99.3	100
authoritative	au'thoritative		0.7	0
		authori'tative	99.3	100
ceremony	'ceremony		3.3	2.65
		ce'remony	96.7	97.35
category	'category		1.3	1.98
		ca'tegory	98.7	98

favouritism	'favouritism		0	0.7
		favou'ritism	100	99.3
journalism	'journalism		1.98	1.3
		jour'nalism	98	98.7
nepotism	'nepotism		0.7	0.7
		ne'potism	99.3	99.3
referee	refe'ree		18.54	17.22
		'referee	81.46	82.78
jubilee	'jubilee		0	0
		jubi'lee	100	100
Vivian	'Vivian		13.91	17.88
		Vi'vian	86.09	82.12
Eunice	'Eunice		15.89	21.19
		Eu'nice	84.11	78.81
Helen	'Helen		18.54	23.84
		He'len	81.46	76.16

Appendix 4: Percentages of SBE and CamE variants in the speech of the different age groups
Phonological style: WLS
Total number of informants: 200
Number of informants per category: 50

Items	Variants		12-19	20-30	31-49	Above 49
	SBE	CamE	%	%	%	%
cupboard	cupd[ə]d		0	0	6	2
		cupd[ɔ]d	100	100	84	94
		cupd[ʌ]d	0	0	10	4
hardworking	hardw[ɔː]ing		0	4	8	8
		hardw[ɔ]ing	98	74	56	88
		hardw[e]ing	0	22	32	2
		hardw[ə]ing	2	0	4	2
drugs	dr[ʌ]gs		0	6	4	8
		dr[ɔ]gs	100	94	96	92
Mary	M[ɛə]ry		0	0	6	6
		M[eɪ]ry	2	4	2	8
		M[e]ry	98	96	92	86
chairs	ch[ɛə]s		0	2	6	2
		ch[iə]s	82	84	94	90
		ch[iɛ]s	10	6	0	2
		ch[ie]s	8	8	0	6
period	p[ɪə]riod		0	0	0	0
		p[i]riod	100	98	84	98
		p[ie]riod	0	2	16	2
mere	m[ɪə]		0	2	6	2
		m[ɛ]	76	82	78	90
		m[ei]	24	16	16	8

village	vill[i]ge		0	0	0	2
		vill[e]ge	100	100	100	98
satan	s[eɪ]tan		2	4	8	8
		s[a]tan	92	80	64	70
		s[ɛ]tan	6	16	28	22
laudable	l[ɔ:]dable		0	0	10	2
		l[au]dable	100	100	90	98
aren't	[ɑ:nt]		0	2	8	4
		[arənt]	78	70	70	64
		[arɛnt]	22	28	22	32
create	cr[i:eɪ]te		0	2	8	12
		cr[ei]te	90	76	66	62
		cr[e]te	10	22	26	26
recent	r[i:]cent		2	6	12	12
		r[e]cent	90	72	66	80
		r[ɛ]cent	8	22	22	8
singing	si[ŋɪŋ]		0	6	14	10
		si[ngin]	100	94	86	90
legal	l[i:]gal		10	14	22	20
		l[e]gal	90	86	78	80
penal	p[i:]nal		0	2	10	6
		p[e]nal	96	94	80	70
		p[ɛ]nal	4	4	10	24
castle	cas[ø]le		36	48	58	50
		cas[t]le	64	52	42	50
pestle	pes[ø]le		12	28	66	36
		pes[t]le	88	72	34	64
bosom	b[ʊ]som		0	0	4	0
		b[ɔ]som	100	100	96	100
tour	t[uə]		0	6	8	2
		t[ɔ]	100	94	92	98
Joan	J[əʊ]n		4	26	32	12
		J[ɔa]n	96	74	68	88
said	sai[d]		0	2	0	4
		sai[t]	100	98	100	96
liquid	liqui[d]		2	12	8	4
		liqui[t]	98	88	92	96
of	o[v]		0	0	0	0
		o[f]	100	100	100	100
bad	ba[d]		4	12	10	10
		ba[t]	96	88	90	90
bag	ba[g]		4	10	4	6
		ba[k]	96	90	96	94
dog	do[g]		0	0	6	4
		do[k]	100	100	94	96
basic	ba[s]ic		8	8	12	6

Word	Variant				
	ba[z]ic	92	92	88	94
consumption	com[s]umption	0	8	12	8
	com[z]umption	100	92	88	92
nursery	nur[s]ery	0	2	2	0
	nur[z]ery	100	98	98	100
December	De[s]ember	2	8	12	8
	De[z]ember	98	92	88	92
conserve	con[s]erve	0	0	2	6
	con[z]erve	100	100	98	94
muscle	mu[s]cle	2	0	10	8
	mu[z]cle	98	100	90	92
increasing	increa[s]ing	0	2	10	10
	increa[z]ing	100	98	90	90
president	pre[z]ident	0	2	6	2
	pre[s]ident	100	98	94	98
Joseph	Jo[z]eph	0	0	2	0
	Jo[s]eph	100	100	98	100
visitor	v[z]itor	0	2	6	4
	v[s]itor	100	98	94	96
position	po[z]ition	2	0	0	4
	po[s]ition	98	100	100	94
reside	re[z]ide	0	0	2	2
	re[s]ide	100	100	98	98
clumsy	clum[z]y	4	8	8	6
	clum[s]y	96	92	92	94
opposite	oppo[z]ite	0	0	10	10
	oppo[s]ite	100	100	90	90
maximum	ma[ks]imum	0	2	4	4
	ma[gz]imum	4	0	6	4
	ma[kz]imum	96	98	90	92
flexible	fl[ks]ible	4	4	6	4
	fl[gz]ible	6	4	4	4
	fl[kz]ible	90	92	90	92
exodus	e[ks]odus	0	0	4	0
	e[gz]odus	10	22	10	18
	e[kz]odus	90	78	86	82
fuel	f[jʊ]el	4	8	8	2
	f[u]el	96	92	92	98
population	pop[jʊ]lation	0	0	4	4
	pop[u]lation	100	100	96	96
journalist	journalis[t]	26	46	58	60
	journalis[ø]	74	54	62	40
typist	typsi[t]	20	30	30	22
	typis[ø]	80	70	70	78
first	firs[t]	16	22	32	28
	firs[ø]	84	78	68	74

post office	pos[t] office		10	24	30	24
		pos[ø] office	90	76	70	76
post office	p[əʊ]st office		0	8	12	6
		p[o]st office	100	92	86	94
		p[u]st office	0	0	2	0
post office	[p]ost office		100	100	100	100
		[b]ost office	0	0	0	0
success	s[ə]ccess		0	4	4	6
		s[ɔ]ccess	100	96	96	94
happy	h[æ]ppy		0	0	2	0
		h[a]ppy	100	100	98	100
sad	sa[d]		2	0	6	16
		sa[t]	98	100	94	84
commented	'commented		0	0	2	0
		com'mented	100	100	98	100
combat	'combat		0	2	6	6
		com'bat	100	98	94	94
colleague	'colleague		0	2	10	4
		col'league	100	98	90	96
challenging	'challenging		0	0	2	0
		chal'lenging	100	100	98	100
ancestors	'ancestors		2	6	12	12
		an'cestors	98	94	88	88
purchase	'purchase		0	0	4	4
		pur'chase	100	100	96	96
success	suc'cess		2	6	6	12
		'success	98	94	94	88
advice	advice		10	12	12	6
		'advice	90	88	88	94
biased	'biased		2	6	8	6
		bi'ased	98	94	92	94
interesting	'interesting		0	2	8	14
		inte'resting	100	98	92	86
embarrass	em'barrass		0	0	4	2
		embar'rass	100	100	96	98
however	how'ever		0	0	2	0
		'however	100	100	98	100
insurance	in'surance		0	0	2	0
		'insurance	100	100	98	100
illogical	il'logical		0	0	2	0
		'illogical	100	100	98	100
irrelevant	ir'relevant		0	2	2	0
		'irrelevant	100	98	98	100
impossible	im'possible		0	4	2	4
		'impossible	100	96	98	98
classified	'classified		0	4	14	4

		classi'fied	100	96	86	96
satisfied	'satisfied		0	6	10	4
		satis'fied	100	92	90	96
criticised	'criticised		2	12	2	2
		criti'cised	98	88	98	98
diversified	di'versified		0	0	4	2
		diversi'fied	100	90	64	82
		'diversified	0	10	32	16
preparatory	pre'paratory		0	0	2	0
		prepa'ratory	100	100	98	100
explanatory	ex'planatory		0	0	2	0
		expla'natory	100	100	98	100
authoritative	au'thoritative		0	0	2	0
		authori'tative	100	100	98	100
ceremony	'ceremony		0	4	8	6
		ce'remony	100	96	92	94
category	'category		0	2	8	8
		ca'tegory	100	98	92	92
favouritism	'favouritism		0	0	2	0
		favou'ritism	100	100	98	100
journalism	'journalism		0	0	12	10
		jour'nalism	100	100	88	90
nepotism	'nepotism		0	0	6	0
		ne'potism	100	100	94	100
referee	refe'ree		36	2	2	22
		referee	64	98	98	78
jubilee	'jubilee		0	0	0	0
		jubi'lee	100	100	100	100
Vivian	'Vivian		2	10	32	26
		Vi'vian	98	90	68	74
Eunice	'Eunice		8	18	14	12
		Eu'nice	92	82	86	88
Helen	'Helen		2	6	22	14
		He'len	98	94	78	86

Appendix 5: Percentages of SBE and CamE variants in the speech of speakers from different occupational groups

Phonological style: WLS

Total number of informant: 60

Number of informants of per category: 15

Items	Variants SBE	Variants CamE	English teachers %	Medical doctors %	Teachers of other disciplines %	Journalists %
cupboard	cupb[ə]d		0	0	0	0
		cupb[ɔ]d	86.7	100	100	66.7
		cupb[ʌ]d	13.3	0	0	33.3
hardworking	hardw[ɔ:]ing		6.7	0	0	20
		hardw[ɔ]ing	60	93.3	100	66.7
		hardw[e]ing	33.3	6.7	0	13.3
		hardw[ə]ing	0	0	0	0
drugs	dr[ʌ]gs		0	0	0	20
		dr[ɔ]gs	100	100	100	80
Mary	M[ɛə]ry		6.7	0	0	0
		M[eɪ]ry	0	0	6.7	20
		M[e]ry	93.3	100	93.3	80
chairs	ch[ɛə]s		20	0	0	40
		ch[iə]s	46.7	40	53.3	33.3
		ch[iɛ]s	0	0	13.3	6.7
		ch[ie]s	33.3	60	33.3	20
period	p[ɪə]riod		0	0	0	0
		p[i]riod	93.3	100	100	100
		p[ie]riod	6.7	0	0	0
mere	m[ɪə]		6.7	0	0	20
		m[ɛ]	80	86.7	100	53.3
		m[ei]	13.3	13.3	0	26.7
village	vill[i]ge		0	0	0	0
		vill[e]ge	100	100	100	100
satan	s[eɪ]tan		13.3	6.7	6.7	40
		s[a]tan	73.3	93.3	86.7	33.3
		s[ɛ]tan	13.3	0	6.7	26.7
laudable	l[ɔ:]deble		13.3	0	0	6.7
		l[au]deble	86.7	100	100	93.3
aren't	[ɑ:nt]		20	0	0	13,3
		[arənt]	60	93.3	100	46.7
		[arent]	20	6.7	0	40
create	cr[i:eɪ]te		26.7	13.3	13.3	20
		cr[ei]te	66.7	86.7	80	80
		cr[e]te	6.7	0	6.7	0
recent	r[i:]cent		40	20	26.7	53.3

		r[e]cent	53.3	80	73.3	40
		r[ɛ]cent	6.7	0	0	6.7
singing	si[ŋɪŋ]		20	0	0	6.7
		si[ngin]	80	100	100	93.3
legal	l[i:]gal		33.3	0	6.7	46.7
		l[e]gal	66.7	100	93.3	53.3
penal	p[i:]nal		20	0	0	6.7
		p[e]nal	73.3	100	100	86.7
		p[ɛ]nal	6.7	0	0	6.7
castle	cas[ø]le		86.7	40	53.3	100
		cas[t]le	13.3	60	46.7	0
pestle	pes[ø]le		73.3	33.3	33.3	93.3
		pes[t]le	26.7	66.7	66.7	6.7
bosom	b[ʊ]som		6.7	0	0	0
		b[ɔ]som	93.3	100	100	100
tour	t[ʊə]		0	0	0	6.7
		t[ɔ]	100	100	100	93.3
visitor	v[z]itor		26.7	0	20	33.3
		v[s]itor	73.3	100	80	66.7
position	po[z]ition		6.7	0	0	0
		po[s]ition	93.3	100	100	100
reside	re[z]die		13.3	0	0	26.7
		re[s]die	86.7	100	100	73.3
clumsy	clum[z]y		6.7	6.7	0	20
		clum[s]y	93.3	93.3	100	80
opposite	oppo[z]ite		6.7	6.7	0	13.3
		oppo[s]ite	93.3	93.3	100	86.7
maximum	ma[ks]imum		6.7	0	0	20
		ma[gz]imum	13.3	0	0	6.7
		ma[kz]imum	80	100	100	73.3
flexible	fle[ks]ible		0	0	0	13.3
		fle[gz]ible	6.7	0	13.3	6.7
		fle[kz]ible	93.3	100	86.7	80
consumption	con[s]umption		13.3	0	0	6.7
		con[z]umption	86.7	100	100	93.3
nursery	nur[s]ery		13.3	6.7	0	20
		nur[z]ery	86.7	93.3	100	80
December	De[s]ember		33.3	0	0	20
		De[z]ember	66.7	100	100	80
conserve	con[s]erve		13.3	0	0	20
		con[z]erve	86.7	100	100	80
muscle	mu[s]cle		6.7	0	6.7	20
		mu[z]cle	93.3	100	93.3	80
increasing	increa[s]ing		6.7	0	0	0
		increa[z]ing	93.3	100	100	100
president	pre[z]ident		0	0	0	6.7

Word						
		pre[s]ident	100	100	100	93.3
Joseph	Jo[z]eph		6.7	6.7	0	13.3
		Jo[s]eph	93.3	93.3	100	86.3
Joan	J[əʊ]n		40	0	6.7	40
		J[ɔa]n	60	100	93.3	60
said	sai[d]		6.7	0	0	6.7
		sai[t]	93.3	100	100	93.3
liquid	liqui[d]		20	13.3	20	33.3
		liqui[t]	80	86.7	80	66.7
of	o[v]		0	0	0	0
		o[f]	100	100	100	100
bad	ba[d]		13.3	0	0	20
		ba[t]	86.7	100	100	80
bag	ba[g]		13.3	0	0	26.3
		ba[k]	86.7	100	100	73.3
dog	do[g]		13.3	6.7	0	20
		do[k]	86.7	93.3	100	80
basic	ba[s]ic		6.7	0	0	13.3
		ba[z]ic	93.3	100	100	86.7
exodus	e[ks]odus		0	0	0	13.3
		e[gz]odus	13.3	26.7	0	0
		e[kz]odus	86.7	73.3	100	86.7
fuel	f[jʊ]el		20	0	6.7	33.3
		f[u]el	80	100	93.3	66.7
population	pop[jʊ]lation		13.3	6.7	6.7	26.7
		pop[u]lation	86.7	93.3	93.3	73.3
journalist	journalis[t]		100	20	73.3	100
		journalis[ø]	0	80	26.7	0
typist	typis[t]		80	26.7	46.7	100
		typis[ø]	20	73.3	53.3	0
first	firs[t]		73.3	26.7	60	93.3
		firs[ø]	26.7	73.3	40	6.7
post office	pos[t] office		40	20	13.3	60
		pos[ø] office	60	80	86.7	40
post office	p[əʊ]st office		20	0	0	33.3
		p[o]st office	80	100	100	66.7
		p[u]st office	0	0	0	0
post office	[p]ost office		100	100	100	100
		[b]ost office	0	0	0	0
success	s[ə]ccess		6.7	0	0	13.3
		s[ɔ]ccess	93.3	100	100	86.7
happy	h[æ]ppy		0	0	0	0
		h[a]ppy	100	100	100	100
sad	sa[d]		26.7	0	13.3	40
		sa[t]	73.3	100	86.7	60
commented	'commented		0	0	0	0

		com'mented	100	100	100	100
combat	'combat		13.3	0	0	40
		com'bat	86.7	100	100	60
colleague	'colleague		20	0	6.7	33.3
		col'league	80	100	93.3	66.7
challenging	'challenging		13.3	0	0	13.3
		chal'lenging	86.7	100	100	86.7
ancestor	'ancestor		26.7	13.3	13.3	40
		an'cestor	73.3	86.7	86.7	60
purchase	'purchase		6.7	0	0	20
		pur'chase	93.3	100	100	80
success	suc'cess		26.7	0	0	26.7
		'success	73.3	100	100	73.3
advice	ad'vice		40	0	6.7	33.3
		'advice	60	100	93.3	66.7
biased	'biased		20	0	13.3	33.3
		bi'ased	80	100	86.7	66.7
interesting	'interesting		26.7	13.3	0	46.7
		inte'resting	73.3	86.7	100	53.3
embarrass	em'barrass		0	0	0	6.7
		embar'rass	100	100	100	93.3
however	how'ever		13.3	0	6.7	6.7
		'however	86.7	100	93.3	93.3
insurance	in'surance		0	0	0	0
		'insurance	100	100	100	100
illogical	il'logical		0	0	0	0
		'illogical	100	100	100	100
irrelevant	ir'relevant		0	0	0	0
		'irrelevant	100	100	100	100
impossible	im'possible		20	0	0	20
		'impossible	80	100	100	80
classified	'classified		26.7	13.3	6.7	46.7
		classi'fied	73.3	86.7	93.3	53.3
satisfied	'satisfied		33.3	13.3	0	60
		satis'fied	66.7	86.7	100	40
criticised	'criticised		46.7	20	13.3	60
		criti'cised	53.3	80	86.7	40
diversified	di'versified		0	0	0	6,7
		diversi'fied	80	100	100	53.3
		'diversified	20	0	0	40
preparatory	pre'paratory		0	0	0	0
		prepa'ratory	100	100	100	100
explanatory	ex'planatory		0	0	0	0
		expla'natory	100	100	100	100
authoritative	au'thoritative		0	0	0	0
		authori'tative	100	100	100	100

ceremony	'ceremony		13.3	0	0	33.3
		ce'remony	86.7	100	100	66.7
category	'category		20	6.7	0	46.7
		ca'tegory	80	93.3	100	53.3
favouritism	'favouritism		6.7	0	0	33.3
		favou'ritism	93.3	100	100	66.7
journalism	'journalism		26.7	6.7	0	60
		jour'nalism	73.3	93.3	100	40
nepotism	'nepotism		6.7	0	0	20
		nepotism	93.3	100	100	80
referee	refe'ree		26.7	13.3	20	13.3
		'referee	73.3	86.7	80	86.7
jubilee	'jubilee		0	0	0	0
		jubi'lee	100	100	100	100
Vivian	'Vivian		46.7	6.7	13.3	73.3
		Vi'vian	53.3	93.3	86.7	26.7
Eunice	'Eunice		60	20	20	80
		Eu'nice	40	80	80	20
Helen	'Helen		73.3	33.3	20	66.7
		He'len	26.7	66.7	80	33.3

Appendix 6: Percentages of phonological variants in the speech of urban and rural speakers

Phonological style: Word List Style

Total number of informants: 200

Number of informants per each regional group: 100

	Variants		Urban speakers	Rural speakers
Items	SBE	CamE	%	%
cupboard	cupb[ə]d		0	0
		cupb[ɔ]d	95	100
		cupb[ʌ]d	5	0
hardworking	hardw[ɔ:]ing		5	2
		hardw[ɔ]ing	70	95
		hardw[e]ing	21	2
		hardw[ə]ing	4	1
drugs	dr[ʌ]gs		2	3
		dr[ɔ]gs	98	97

Mary	M[εə]ry		0	0
		M[eɪ]ry	4	1
		M[e]ry	96	99
chairs	ch[εə]s		1	0
		ch[iə]s	92	99
		ch[iɛ]s	4	1
		ch[ie]s	3	0
period	p[ɪə]riod		0	0
		p[i]riod	94	100
		p[ie]riod	6	0
mere	m[ɪə]		1	1
		m[ɛ]	97	99
		m[ei]	2	0
village	vill[i]ge		0	0
		vill[e]ge	100	100
satan	s[eɪ]tan		5	6
		s[a]tan	87	92
		s[ɛ]tan	8	2
laudable	l[ɔ:]dable		2	0
		l[au]dable	98	100
aren't	[ɑːnt]		3	0
		[arənt]	92	99
		[arɛnt]	5	1
create	cr[iːeɪ]te		0	2
		cr[ei]te	89	95
		cr[e]te	11	3
recent	r[iː]cent		3	4
		r[e]cent	78	85
		r[ɛ]cent	19	11
singing	si[ŋɪŋ]		5	1
		si[ngin]	95	99
legal	l[iː]gal		6	6
		l[e]gal	94	94
penal	p[iː]nal		3	0
		p[e]nal	89	97
		p[ɛ]nal	8	3
castle	cas[ø]le		13	7
		cas[t]le	87	93
pestle	pes[ø]le		15	10
		pes[t]le	87	90
bosom	b[ʊ]som		1	0
		b[ɔ]som	99	100
tour	t[uə]		3	5
		t[ɔ]	97	95
Joan	J[əʊ]n		8	6
		J[ɔa]n	92	94

said	sai[d]		0	0
		sai[t]	100	100
liquid	liqui[d]		5	2
		liqui[t]	95	98
of	o[v]		0	0
		o[f]	100	100
bad	ba[d]		2	0
		ba[t]	98	100
bag	ba[g]		2	5
		ba[k]	98	95
dog	do[g]		0	1
		do[k]	100	99
basic	ba[s]ic		4	6
		ba[z]ic	96	94
consumption	com[s]umption		7	3
		com[z]umption	93	97
nursery	nur[s]ery		1	0
		nur[z]ery	99	100
December	De[s]ember		2	0
		De[z]ember	98	100
conserve	con[s]erve		0	2
		con[z]erve	100	98
muscle	mu[s]cle		8	2
		mu[z]cle	92	98
increasing	increa[s]ing		4	5
		increa[z]ing	96	95
president	pre[z]ident		1	0
		pre[s]ident	99	100
Joseph	Jo[z]eph		0	0
		Jo[s]eph	100	100
visitor	v[z]itor		2	2
		v[s]itor	98	98
position	po[z]ition		0	1
		po[s]ition	100	99
reside	re[z]ide		0	0
		re[s]ide	100	100
clumsy	clum[z]y		3	2
		clum[s]y	97	98
opposite	oppo[z]ite		1	2
		oppo[s]ite	99	98
maximum	ma[ks]imum		5	4
		ma[gz]imum	10	23
		ma[kz]imum	85	73
flexible	fl[ks]ible		11	10
		fl[gz]ible	8	2
		fl[kz]ible	81	88

exodus	e[ks]odus		4	3
		e[gz]odus	11	10
		e[kz]odus	85	87
fuel	f[ju]el		1	2
		f[u]el	99	98
population	pop[ju]lation		4	0
		pop[u]lation	96	100
journalist	journalis[t]		28	36
		journalis[ø]	72	64
typist	typis[t]		31	36
		typis[ø]	69	64
first	firs[t]		29	26
		firs[ø]	71	74
post office	pos[t] office		8	13
		pos[ø] office	92	87
post office	p[ɔʊ]st office		5	6
		p[o]st office	95	94
		p[u]st office	0	0
post office	[p]ost office		100	100
		[b]ost office	0	0
success	s[ə]ccess		1	0
		s[ɔ]ccess	99	100
happy	h[æ]ppy		0	0
		h[a]ppy	100	100
sad	sa[d]		3	3
		sa[t]	97	97
commented	'commented		2	0
		com'mented	98	100
combat	'combat		8	5
		com'bat	92	95
colleague	'colleague		2	0
		col'league	98	100
challenging	'challenging		3	1
		chal'lenging	97	99
ancestors	'ancestors		7	4
		an'cestors	93	96
purchase	'purchase		2	0
		pur'chase	98	100
success	suc'cess		6	3
		'success	94	97
advice	ad'vice		11	6
		'advice	89	94
biased	'biased		2	1
		bi'ased	98	99
interesting	'interesting		3	4
		inte'resting	97	96

embarrass	em'barrass		0	0
		embar'rass	100	100
however	how'ever		1	0
		'however	99	100
insurance	in'surance		0	0
		'insurance	100	100
illogical	il'logical		0	0
		'illogical	100	100
irrelevant	ir'relevant		0	0
		'irrelevant	100	100
impossible	im'possible		1	0
		'impossible	99	100
classified	'classified		2	1
		classi'fied	98	99
satisfied	'satisfied		1	1
		satis'fied	99	99
criticised	'criticised		3	0
		criti'cised	97	100
diversified	di'versified		0	0
		diversi'fied	96	100
		'diversified	4	0
preparatory	pre'paratory		0	0
		prepa'ratory	100	100
explanatory	ex'planatory		0	0
		expla'natory	100	100
authoritative	au'thoritative		1	0
		authori'tative	99	100
ceremony	'ceremony		4	4
		ce'remony	96	96
category	'category		4	2
		ca'tegory	96	98
favouritism	'favouritism		1	0
		favou'ritism	99	100
journalism	'journalism		1	2
		jour'nalism	99	98
nepotism	'nepotism		2	0
		ne'potism	98	100
referee	refe'ree		4	6
		referee	96	94
jubilee	'jubilee		0	0
		jubi'lee	100	100
Vivian	'Vivian		11	4
		Vi'vian	89	96
Eunice	'Eunice		13	5
		Eu'nice	87	95

Appendix 7: Percentages of SBE and CamE variants in the speech of speakers from different ethnic groups

Phonological style: WLS

Total number of informants: 300

Number of informants per ethnic group: 60

items	Variants SBE	Variants CamE	Bafut %	Banso %	Bamileke %	Bangwa %	Bakweri %
cupboard	cupb[ə]d		1.7	1.7	3.3	0	3.3
		cupb[ɔ]d	95	98.3	95	98.3	96.7
		cupb[ʌ]d	3.3	0	1.7	1.7	0
hardworking	hardw[ɜ:]ing		3.3	0	6.7	0	0
		hardw[ɔ]ing	83.3	90	70	91.7	81.7
		hardw[e]ing	11.7	10	3.3	0	16.7
		hardw[ə]ing	1.7	0	20	8.3	1.7
drugs	dr[ʌ]gs		3.3	3.3	1.7	0	5
		dr[ɔ]gs	96.7	96.7	98.3	100	95
Mary	M[ɛə]ry		0	1.7	1.7	3.3	0
		M[eɪ]ry	1.7	3.3	1.7	1.7	3.3
		M[e]ry	98.3	95	96.7	95	96.7
chairs	Ch[ɛə]s		0	0	1.7	0	1.7
		ch[iə]s	93.3	96.7	95	98.3	96.7
		ch[iɛ]s	3.3	1.7	3.3	1.7	0
		ch[ie]s	3.3	1.7	0	0	1.7
period	p[ɪə]riod		0	0	1.7	0	0
		p[i]riod	100	96.7	95	98.3	98,3
		p[ie]riod	0	3.3	3.3	1.7	1.7
mere	m[ɪə]		0	0	3.3	1.7	3.3
		m[ɛ]	96.7	98.3	100	96.7	95
		m[ei]	3.3	1.7	0	1.7	1.7
village	vill[i]ge		0	0	0	0	0
		vill[e]ge	100	100	100	100	100
satan	s[eɪ]tan		1.7	0	5	1,7	1,7
		s[a]tan	95	95	85	95	93.3
		s[ɛ]tan	3.3	5	10	3.3	5
laudable	l[ɔ:]deble		1.7	1.7	6.7	0	0
		l[au]deble	98.3	98.3	93.3	100	100
aren't	[ɑːnt]		0	0	1.7	1.7	0
		[arənt]	48.3	60	58,3	55	51.7
		[arɛnt]	51.7	40	40	43,3	48,3
create	cr[iːeɪ]te		0	0	1.7	0	0
		cr[ei]te	78.3	83.3	8 1.7	88.3	70
		cr[e]te	12.7	16.7	16.7	11.7	30
recent	r[iː]cent		5	1.7	1.7	1.7	3.3
		r[ːe]cent	88.3	91.7	93.3	90	93.3

	r[ɛ]cent	6.7	6.7	5	8.3	3.3
singing	si[ŋɪŋ]	3.3	6.7	1.7	1.7	3.3
	si[ngin]	96.7	93.3	98.3	98.3	96.7
legal	l[i:]gal	11.7	5	6.7	5	6.7
	l[e]gal	88.3	95	93.3	95	93.3
penal	p[i:]nal	5	10	5	5	10
	p[e]nal	88.3	86.7	86,7	81,7	85
	p[ɛ]nal	6.7	3.3	8,3	13,3	5
castle	cas[ø]le	20	18.3	18,3	23,3	18,3
	cas[t]le	80	81.7	81,7	76,7	81,7
pestle	pes[ø]le	35	30	26,7	30	31,7
	pes[t]le	65	70	73,3	70	68,3
bosom	b[ʊ]som	0	1.7	5	0	0
	b[ɔ]som	100	98,3	95	100	100
tour	t[ʊə]	1.7	3.3	8,3	5	5
	t[ɔ]	98.3	96.7	91,7	95	95
visitor	v[z]itor	0	0	1,7	0	3,3
	v[s]itor	100	100	98,3	100	96,7
position	po[z]ition	0	0	5	1,7	1,7
	po[s]ition	100	100	95	98,3	98,3
reside	re[z]die	0	0	3,3	0	0
	re[s]die	100	100	96,7	100	100
clumsy	clum[z]y	6.7	10	10	6,7	8,3
	clum[s]y	93.3	90	90	93,3	91,7
opposite	oppo[z]ite	10	0	8,3	0	3,3
	oppo[s]ite	90	100	91,7	100	96,7
maximum	ma[ks]imum	1.7	5	6,7	1,7	0
	ma[gz]i-mum	31.7	40	26,6	28,3	20
	ma[kz]i-mum	66.7	55	55	70	80
flexible	fle[ks]ible	13.3	5	3,3	3,3	3,3
	fle[gz]ible	6.7	18.3	16,7	20	23,3
	fle[kz]ible	80	76.7	80	76,7	73,3
consumption	con[s]umption	6.7	0	3,3	3,3	3,3
	con[z]umption	93.3	100	96,7	96,7	98,3
nursery	nur[s]ery	0	0	3,3	0	0
	nur[z]ery	100	100	96,7	100	100
December	De[s]ember	8.3	8.3	11,7	11,7	10
	De[z]ember	91.7	91.7	88,3	88,3	90
conserve	con[s]erve	5	5	3,3	3,3	6,7
	con[z]erve	95	95	96,7	96,7	93,3
muscle	mu[s]cle	8.3	5	10	11,7	11,7
	mu[z]cle	91.7	95	90	88,3	88,3
increasing	increa[s]ing	1.7	0	6,7	0	1,7
	increa[z]ing	98.3	100	93,3	100	98,3
president	pre[z]ident	0	1.7	1,7	0	0

		pre[s]ident	100	98.3	98,3	100	100
Joseph	Jo[z]eph		0	0	1,7	0	0
		Jo[s]eph	100	100	98,3	100	100
Joan	J[əʊ]n		21.7	18.3	13,3	15	21,7
	J[ɔa]n		78.3	81.7	86,7	85	78,3
said	sai[d]		0	0	0	0	1,7
		sai[t]	100	100	100	100	98,3
liquid	liqui[d]		3.3	1.7	3,3	1,7	5
		liqui[t]	96.7	98.3	96,7	98,3	95
Of	o[v]		0	0	0	0	0
		o[f]	100	100	100	100	100
bad	ba[d]		0	1.7	6,7	0	0
		ba[t]	100	98.3	93,3	100	100
bag	bag]		3.3	0	3,3	0	1,7
		ba[k]	96.7	100	96,7	100	98,3
dog	do[g]		0	0	6,7	0	0
		do[k]	100	100	93,3	100	100
basic	ba[s]ic		8.3	6.7	5	5	3,3
		ba[z]ic	91.7	93.3	95	95	96,7
exodus	e[ks]odus		3.3	8.3	8,3	0	0
		e[gz]odus	25	28.3	48,3	33,3	58,3
		e[kz]odus	71.7	63.3	43,3	66,7	41,7
fuel	f[jʊ]el		0	0	6,7	1,7	1,7
		f[u]el	100	100	93,3	98,3	98,3
population	pop[jʊ]lation	pop[u]lation	5	1.7	3,3	1,7	1,7
			95	98.3	96,7	98,3	98,3
journalist	journalis[t]		18.3	16.7	21,7	23,3	18,3
		journalis[ø]	81.7	83.3	70	76,7	81,7
typist	typis[t]		13.3	21.7	13,3	23,3	16,7
		typis[ø]	86.7	78.3	86,7	76,7	83,3
first	firs[t]		18.3	21.7	33,33	21,7	18,3
		firs[ø]	81.7	78.3	70	78,3	81,7
post office	pos[t] office		16.7	13.3	18,33	18,3	18,3
		pos[ø] office	83.3	86.7	71,7	81,7	81,7
post office	p[əʊ]st office		8.3	6.7	5	5	10
		p[o]st office	91.7	91.7	95	95	90
		p[u]ost office	0	1.7	0	0	0
post office	[p]ost office		100	100	100	100	100
		[b]ost office	0	0	0	0	0
success	s[ə]ccess		5	5	1,7	0	0
		s[ɔ]ccess	95	95	98,3	100	100
happy	h[æ]ppy		0	1.7	1,7	0	0
		h[a]ppy	100	98.3	98,3	100	100
Sad	sa[d]		3.3	1.7	3,3	1,7	0
		sa[t]	96.7	98.3	96,7	98,3	100
commented	'commented		0	1.7	1,7	0	0

		com'mented	100	98.3	98,3	100	100
combat	'combat		10	18.3	10	16,7	18,3
		com'bat	90	81.7	90	83,3	81,7
colleague	'colleague		1.7	0	3,3	0	0
		col'league	98.3	100	96,7	100	100
challenging	'challenging		3.3	3.3	8,3	3,3	8,3
		chal'lenging	96.7	96.7	91,7	96,7	91,7
ancestor	'ancestor		11.7	5	11,7	10	6,7
		an'cestor	88.3	95	88,3	90	93,3
purchase	'purchase		0	5	8,3	5	8,3
		pur'chase	100	95	91,7	95	91,7
success	suc'cess		13.3	8.3	6,7	5	8,3
		'success	86.7	91.7	93,3	95	91,7
advice	ad'vice		20	10	10	8,3	11,7
		'advice	80	90	90	91,7	88,3
biased	'biased		0	0	5	1,7	1,7
		bi'ased	100	100	95	98,3	98,3
interesting	'interesting		3.3	1.7	1,7	1,7	3,3
		inte'resting	96.7	98.3	98,3	98,3	96,7
embarrass	em'barrass		0	0	1,7	0	0
		embar'rass	100	100	98,3	100	100
however	how'ever		1.7	0	1,7	0	0
		'however	98.3	100	98,3	100	100
insurance	in'surance		0	0	0	0	0
		'insurance	100	100	100	100	100
illogical	il'logical		0	0	3,3	0	0
		'illogical	100	100	96,7	100	100
irrelevant	ir'relevant		0	0	1,7	0	0
		'irrelevant	100	100	98,3	100	100
impossible	im'possible		0	1.7	3,3	0	0
		'impossible	100	98.3	96,7	100	100
classified	'classified		1.7	0	6,7	1,7	0
		classi'fied	98.3	100	93,3	98,3	100
satisfied	'satisfied		1.7	3.3	8,3	1,7	1,7
		satis'fied	98.3	96.7	91,7	98,3	98,3
criticised	'criticised		1.7	1.7	6,7	0	0
		criti'cised	98.3	98.3	93,3	100	100
diversified	di'versified		0	0	1,7	0	0
		diversi'fied	96.7	100	81,7	98,3	95
		'diversified	3.3	0	16,7	1,7	5
preparatory	pre'paratory		0	0	1,7	0	0
		prepa'ratory	100	100	98,3	100	100
explanatory	ex'planatory		0	0	1,7	0	0
		expla'natory	100	100	98,3	100	100
authoritative	au'thoritative		0	0	1,7	0	0
		authori'tative	100	100	98,3	100	100

ceremony	'ceremony		6.7	5	5	6,7	5
		ce'remony	93.3	95	95	93,3	95
category	'category		1.7	3.3	3,3	0	0
		ca'tegory	98.3	96.7	96,7	100	100
favouritism	'favouritism		0	0	1,7	0	0
		favou'ritism	100	100	90	100	100
journalism	'journalism		3.3	0	1,7	0	1,7
		jour'nalism	96.7	100	90	100	98,3
nepotism	'nepotism		0	1.7	1,7	0	0
		ne'potism	100	98.3	90	100	100
referee	refe'ree		6.7	1.7	6,7	0	0
		referee	93.3	98.3	93,3	100	100
jubilee	'jubilee		0	0	0	0	0
		jubi'lee	100	100	100	100	100
Vivian	'Vivian		8.3	11.7	8,3	13,3	10
		Vi'vian	91.7	88.3	91,7	86,7	90
Eunice	'Eunice		10	10	8,3	11,7	15
		Eu'nice	90	90	91,7	88,3	85
Helen	'Helen		6.7	3.3	8,3	5	5
		He'len	93.3	96.7	91,7	95	95

Appendix 8a: A continuous assessment exercise used to evaluate speakers in the different moods.

Ecole Normale Supérieure
Department of English
BL4
8 May 2000

Quiz

Instruction: Any signs of cheating will cause the disqualification of the student's script!

Question: Transcribe the underlined portions of the following words according to Standard British English (SBE) norms: f*oo*t, f*oo*d, b*i*t, b*ea*t, journalis*t*, liqui*d*, bag, cr*ea*te.

Appendix 8b: The speakers' speech in the different categories of mood

	Variants		Mood of anger	Mood of fear	Mood of joy
Items	SBE	CamE	%	%	%
f*oo*t	f[ʊ]t		27.3	36.4	36.4
		f[u]t	72.7	45.6	63.6
f*oo*d	f[u:]d		36.4	27.3	27.3
		f[u]d	63.3	72.7	72.7
b*i*t	b[ɪ]t		27.3	45.5	36.4
		b[i]t	72.7	54.5	63.6
b*ea*t	b[i:]t		36.4	27.3	45.5
		b[i]t	63.6	72.7	54.5
journalis*t*	journalis[t]		36.4	18.2	81.8
		journalis[ø]	63.6	81.8	18.2
liqui*d*	liqui[d]		18.2	9.1	36.4
		liqui[t]	81.8	90.9	63.6
bag	ba[g]		9.1	9.1	36.4
		ba[k]	90.9	90.9	63.6
cr*ea*te	cr[ɪeɪ]te		9.1	9.1	36.4
		cr[ei]te	81.8	90.9	54.5
		cr[e]te	9.1	0	9.1

References

Akere, F. (1980). "Evaluation Criteria for a Local Model of English Pronunciation: An Experimental Study of Attitudes to the Accents of English Used by Africans". In *Lares*, Vol. 1 Pp. 19-39.

Atechi, N. Samuel. 1996. "Some Speech forms of Cameroon Calling Programme in CRTV: A phonological analysis". Unpublished Masters Degree (Maîtrise) thesis, University of Yaounde 1.

Bailey, E.P. and P.A. Powel (1986). *Writing Research Papers*. New York: Longman Inc.

Bailey, G. 1993. "A Perspective on African -America English". In Preston, R. D. (ed.) *American Dialect Research*. Pp. 287-318, Amsterdam: Benjamin's Publishing Co.

Bailey, R. W. and J. L. Robinson. 1973. *Varieties of Present Day English*. New York: Macmillan.

Bakir, Murtadha. 1986. "Sex differences in the approximation of Standard Arabic: A case study". In *Anthropological Linguistics*. Vol. 28, Pp. 3-9.

Bamgbose, Ayo. 1971. "The English Language in Nigeria". In Spencer 1971, Pp. 35-48.

____ (1983)."Standard Nigerian English: Issues of Identification". In Kachru (1983), Pp. 99-109.

Banjo, A. 1971. "Standard of Correctness in Nigerian English". In *West African Journal of Education*, Vol. 15, No.2, Pp. 123-127.

Bansal, R. K. 1969. "The Intelligibility of Indian English". *Monograph 4*. Hyderabad: Central Institute of English and Foreign Languages.

Baugh, John (1993). "Adapting dialectology: The conduct of community Language studies". In Preston, R. D. ed. 1993. *American Dialect Research*. Pp. 167-191, Amsterdam: Benjamin's Publishing Co.

Bernard, J. 1972. *The Sex Game*. New York: Atheneum.

Bobda, A. S. 1986. "Syllable Stress in Cameroon Standard English". In *Annals*, Faculty of Letters, University of Yaounde.

____ 1991. "Does pronunciation matter?". In *English Teaching Forum*. Vol. 29, No. 4. Pp. 28-30.

____ 1993. "English Pronunciation in Cameroon, Conflicts and Consequences". In *Journal of Multilingual and Multicultural Development*, Vol. 14, No. 6, Pp.435-445.

____ 1993. "Testing Pronunciation". In *English Teaching Forum*. Vol. 29, No. 3, Pp. 18-21.

____ and P.N. Mbangwana. 1993. *An Introduction to Spoken English*. Lagos: Lagos University Press.

____ 2002. *Watch Your English!* 2nd ed. Yaounde: B&K Language Institute.

____ 1994. "Teaching English Pronunciation in Cameroon: Problems, Suggestions, and Prospects". In *Syllabus*. Vol. 1, No. 4, Pp. 221-237.

____ 1994. *Aspects of Cameroon English Phonology*. Bern: Peter Lang.

____1997. "Further 'Demystifying word stress'". In *English Today*. Vol. 13, No. 4, Pp. 48-56.

____ April 1999. "Pertinent, but not a contradiction of Kachru". In *English Today*, Vol. 15, No. 2, Pp. 29-30.

____ 2000a. "Comparing some phonological features across African accents of English". In *English Studies*, Vol. 3, Pp 249-226.

____ 2000b. "Explicating the features of African English Pronunciation: some steps further". In *ZAA*, Stauffenburg Verlag.

____ 2000c. "Research on New Englishes: A critical review of some findings so far with a focus on Cameroon English". In *Arbeiten aus Anglistik und Americkanistik (AAA)*, Band 25, Gunter Narr Verlag Tübingen.

___ 2000d. "English Pronunciation in sub-Saharan Africa as illustrated by the NURSE vowel". In *English Today* Vol. 16, No. 4.

Boton, W.F.ed. 1966. *The English Language: Essays by English and American Men of Letters*. Cambridge: Cambridge University Press.

Briscoe, A. M. 1978. *Hormones and gender. Genes and Gender* 1, eds. Ethel Torbach and Betty Rosoff. New York: Gordian Press, Pp. 31-50.

Bright, W. and A. k. Ramanujan. 1964. *Sociolinguistic variation and Language Change*. In Pride, J. B. and J. Holmes. ed. 1972. *Sociolinguistics*. Harmondsworth: Penguin Books Ltd, Pp. 157-166.

Brown, G. 1977. *Listening to Spoken English*. London: Longman

Cameron, D. and J. Coates. 1988. *Some Problems in the Sociolinguistic Explanation of Sex differences*. In *Women in their Speech Communities: New Perspective on Language and Sex*, Cameron, D. and J. Coates. eds. London: Longman, Pp. 13-26.

___ 1988. *Introduction. Women in Their Speech Communities: New Perspective on Language and Sex*," Cameron, D. and J. Coates. eds. London: Longman. Pp. 3-12.

___ ed. 1990. *The Feminist Critique of Language. A Reader*. Longman: Routledge.

___ and J. Coates 1985. "Some problems in the sociolinguistic explanation of sex differences". In *Language and Communication*. Vol. 5, No. 3 Pp. 143-151.

Chambers, J. K. 1995. *Sociolinguistic Theory*. Oxford: Blackwell Inc.

___ "Sociolinguistic Dialectology". In Preston, D. R. ed. 1993. *American Dialect Research*. Amsterdam, Pp. 133-164.

Cheshire, J. 1984. "Language and Sexism". In Trudgill, P. ed. *Application of Sociolinguistics*. London: Academic Press.

___ 1978. *Variation in an English Dialect*.Cambridge: Cambridge University Press

___ ed. 1991. *English Around the World: Sociolinguistic Perspectives*. Cambridge: Cambridge University Press.

Chevillet, F. April 1999. "The ills of EIL". In *English Today*. Vol. 15, No. 2, Pp. 33.

Chomsky, N. 1980. *Rules and Representations*. New York: Columbia University Press.

Chumbow, B. S. and A. S. Bobda. 1996. "The life-cycle of post-imperial English in Cameroon". In Fishman J. A., A. W. Conrad and A. Rubal-Lopez. eds. 1996. *Post-Imperial English: Status Change in Former British and American Colonies, 1940-1990*. Berlin: Mouton de Gruyter.

Coon, D. 1981. *Introduction to Psychology (Exploration and Application)*.California: Stuart Kanter.

Crystal, D. 1985. *Linguistics*. Australia: Edward Arnold Ltd.

Crystal, D. 1987. *The Cambridge Encyclopaedia of Language*.Cambridge: Cambridge University Press.

Crystal, D. 1997. *A Dictionary of Linguistics and Phonetics*. 4th ed. Oxford: Blackwell Publishing Ltd.

Deuchar, M. 1988. "A Pragmatic Account of Women's Use of Standard Speech". In Coates, J. and D. Cameron. eds. *Women in their Speech Communities: New Perspectives on Language and Sex*, Pp. 27-32, London: Longman.

Dunstan. F. ed. 1969. *TWELVE Nigerian Languages. A handbook on their sound systems for teachers of English*. London: Longman.

Eakins, B.W. and R.G. Eakins. 1978. *Sex Differences in Human Communication*. Boston: Houghton Mifflin Company.

Eckert, P. 1980. *Jocks and Burnouts: Social Categories and Identity in the High School*. New York: Teachers' College Press.

___ 1988. *Adolescent Social Structure and the Spread of Linguistic Change*. In *Language in Society*. Vol. 17, Pp. 183-207.

Ferguson, C. A. 1959a. "Diglossia". In *Word*, Vol. 15, Pp. 325-40.

___ 1959b. "The Arabic Koiné". In *Language*, Vol. 35, Pp. 616-630.

___ 1970. "The Role of Arabic in Ethiopia: A sociolinguistic perspective". In *Language and Linguistics*. Monograph Series 23, Pp.355-368.

Fischer, J.L. 1985. "Social Influences on the Choice of a Linguistic Variant". In *Word*, Vol. 14, Pp.47-56.

Flannery, R. 1946. "Men and Women's Speech in Gros Ventre". In *International Journal of American Linguistics*. Vol. 12, Pp. 133-135.

Francia, W. N. 1993. "The Historical and Cultural Interpretation of Dialect". In Preston, R. D. ed. 1993. *American Dialect Research*. Pp. 13-30. Amsterdam: John Benjamin's Publishing Co.

Friel, B. 1988. *Translation*. London: Faber & Faber

Geertz, C. 1960. "Linguistic Etiquette". In Pride, J. B. and Holmes eds. 1972. *Sociolinguistics*, Pp. 167-179. Harmondsworth: Penguin Books Ltd.

Gimson, A. C. 1980. *An Introduction to the Pronunciation of English*. London: ELBS.

Grant, W. 1914. *The Pronunciation of English in Scotland*. Cambridge: Cambridge University Press.

Gumperz, J. ed. 1982. *Language and Social Identity*. Cambridge: Cambridge University Press.

Guy, G. R. 1993. "The quantitative analysis of Linguistic variation". In Preston, R. D. ed. 1993. *American Dialect Research*, Pp. 223-249. Amsterdam: Benjamins Publishing Co.

Habick, Timothy. 1991. "Burnouts versus Rednecks: Effects of Group Membership on the Phonetic System". In Eckert, Penelope ed. 1991. *New Ways of Analysing Sound Change*, Pp. 185-212. San Diego: Academic Press.

Hancock, I. and R. Angogo. 1982. "English in East Africa". In Bailey, R. and M. Gorlach eds. 1982. *English as a World Language*, Pp. 306-323. Ann Arbor.

Hibiya, Junko. 1988. "A Quantitative Study of Tokyo Japanese", Ph.D. dissertation, Department of Linguistics, University of Pennsylvania.

Honey, John. 1989. *Does Accent Matter?* London: Faber and Faber.

___ 1997. *Language is Power: The Story of Standard English and Its Enemies*. London: Faber and Faber.

Horvath, Barbara M. 1985. *Variation in Australian English: The Sociolects of Sydney*. Cambridge: Cambridge University Press.

Hubbell, Alan F. 1950. *The Pronunciation of English in New York City*. New York: Columbia University Press.

Hughes, A. and P. Trudgill. 1979. *English Accents and Dialect*. London: Edward Arnold.

Hymes, D. ed. 1964. *Language in Culture and Society*. New York: Harper International.

Ikonne, Chidi. 1986. "Nigerian English and International Intelligibility: The Situation in the United States of America". In Solomon O. Unoh. ed. 1986. *Use of English in Communication: The Nigerian Experience*, Pp. 23-38. Ibadan: Spectrum Books Limited.

Jankowitz, A. D. 1991. *Business Research Project for Students*. London: Chapman and Hall.

Jennifer, C. 1986. *Women, Men and Language*. New York: Longman Inc.

Jesperson, O. 1921. *Language, Its Nature, Development and Origin*. London: George Allen & Unwin Ltd.

Jibril, M. 1982. "Phonological Variation in Nigerian English", Unpublished Ph.D. dissertation, Lancaster University.

___ "Language in Nigerian Education". In *Indian Journal of Applied Linguistics*, Vol. 13, Pp.38-51.

Kachru, B. B. 1981. "The Pragmatics of Non-native Varieties of English". In Smith 1981, Pp. 15-39.

___ 1983. *The Indianisation of English: The English Language in India*. New Delhi: Oxford University Press.

___ 1983a. "The Other Side of English". In Kachru 1983, Pp. 1-4.

___ 1985. "Standards, Codification and Sociolinguistic Realism: The English Language in the Outer Circle". In R. Quirk and Widdowson. eds., Pp. 11-30.

___ 1986. *The Alchemy of English. The Spread, Function and Models of Non-native Englishes.* Oxford: Pergamon Press.

___ 1992. "World Englishes: Approaches, Issues and Resources". In *Language Teaching.* Vol. 25, No.1, Pp 1-14.

___ ed. 1982. *The Other Tongue: English Across Cultures.* Urnbana: University of Illinois Press.

___ ed. 1983. *The Other Tongue.* Oxford: Pergamon.

___ and Nelson, C. L. (1996). *World Englishes* in Mckay and Horberger (1996), Pp. 71-102.

Kimura, Doreen. 1987. "Are men's and women's brains really different?" In *Canadian Psychology.* Vol. 28, Pp.133-47.

Kouega, J. P. 1991. "Some Characteristics of Cameroon Media News in English. An Explanatory Study of Radio and Television News Text", Unpublished Doctorat de 3e Cycle Thesis, University of Yaounde.

Labov, W. 1964. "Stages in the acquisition of standard English". In Shuy, R. 1964. *Social Dialects and Language Learning,* Pp. 77-103. Illinois-Champaign: National Council of Teachers of English.

___ 1966. *The Social Stratification of English in New York City.* Washington, D. C.: Center for Applied Linguistics.

___ 1969. "The Logic of Non-standard English". In Giglioli. ed. 1972. *Language and Social Context,* Pp. 179-215. Harmonndsworth: Penguin Books Ltd.

___ 1970. "The Study of Language in its Social Context". In Studium Generale, Vol. 23, Pp. 30-87.

___ 1972. *Language in the Inner City.* Philadelphia: University of Pennsylvania Press.

___ 1972. *Sociolinguistic Patterns.* Philadelphia: University of Pennsylvania Press.

Ladefoged, P. 1974. *A Course in Phonetics.* Harcourt: Brace Jovanovich.

Lass, R. 1984. *Phonology: An Introduction to Basic Concepts.* Cambridge: Cambridge University Press.

Littlejohn, J. 1972. *Social Stratification.* London: George Allen & Unwin.

Longman .1987. *Dictionary of Contemporary English.* UK: Longman Group Limited

Lowenberg, P. H. (1993). "Issues of Validity in Tests of English as a World Language: Whose standards?" In *World Englishes.* Vol. 12, No. 1, Pp. 95-106.

Macaulay, R.K.S. 1976. "Social class and Language in Glasgow". In *Language in Society* Vol. 5, Pp. 173-88.

Macaulay, R.K.S. 1977. *Language, Social Class and Education: A Glasgow Study.* Edinburgh: The University Press.

Maccoby, E. E. and C. N. Jacklin. 1974. *The Psychology of Sex Differences.* Stanford: Stanford University Press.

Malmberg, B. 1993. *Phonetics.* New York: Dover Books.

Malmkjar; K. ed. 1991. *The Linguistics Encyclopaedia.* London: Routledge.

Masanga, D.W. 1983. "The Spoken English of Educated Moghamo People: A Phonological Study". Unpublished Doctorat de 3e Cycle thesis, University of Yaounde.

Mbangwana, P. N. 1983. "The Scope and Role of Pidgin English in Cameroon". In Koenig, E. L., E. Chia, Povey. eds. *A Sociolinguistic Profile of Urban Centres in Cameroon,* Pp. 144-162. California: Cross-road Press.

___ 1987. "Some Characteristics of Sound Patterns of Cameroon Standard English." In *Multilingua,* Vol. 4, Pp. 411-424.

___ 1988. "Groundwork in Spoken English". Unpublished mimeograph.

Mbassi-Manga, F. 1973. "English in Cameroon. A study of Historical Contacts, Patterns of Usage and Current Trends". Unpublished Ph.D. dissertation, University of Leeds.

McArthur, T. 1998. *The English Languages*. Cambridge: Cambridge University Press.

McKay, S. L. and N. H. Horberger. eds. 1996. *Sociolinguistics and Language Teaching*. Cambridge: Cambridge University Press.

Milroy, J. and L. Milroy. 1978. "Belfast: Change and Variation in an Urban Vernacular". In Trudgill, P. ed. *Sociolinguistic Patterns in British English*, Pp. 19-36. London: Edward Arnold.

___ and L. Milroy. 1985. *Authority in Language*. London: Routledge.

Modiano, M. 1999a. "International English in the Global Village". In *English Today*, Vol. 15, No. 2, Pp. 22-28.

___ 1999b. "Standard English(es) and Educational Practices for the World's Lingua Franca". In *English Today* Vol. 15, No. 4, Pp. 3-13.

Murray, T. E. 1985. "On solving the dilemma of the Hawthorne effect". Papers from the Fifth International Conference on Methods in Dialectology. Warkentyne, H. J. ed. Victoria, B. C.: Department of Linguistics, University of Victoria.

Newbrook, M. 1982. "Sociolinguistics reflexes of dialect interference in West Wirral". Unpublished Ph.D. dissertation, Reading University.

Ngefac, A. 1997. "The Influence of some sociolinguistic variables on English Pronunciation: A case study of Form 1 and Upper Sixth Students in Anglophone Schools in Yaounde". Unpublished M. A. thesis, University of Yaounde.

___ 2004. "What's happening to Phrasal Verbs in Cameroon?". In Ibadan Journal of Multicultural and Multidisciplinary Studies", vol. 19, no 1, pp 24-33.

___ 2005. "Homophones and Heterophones in Cameroon English". In *Alizés*, no. 25 & 26 , pp. 39-52.

___ 2006a. "Linguistic variants as signals of social hierarchy: The ambiguous situation of Cameroon". In PHiN 35, pp 25-31.

___ and B. M. Sala. 2006b. "Cameroon Pidgin and Cameroon English at a confluence: A real-time investigation". In *English World-Wide*, 27 :2, 217-227.

___ 2006c. "What's happening to Cameroon Pidgin English? The depidginisation of Cameroon Pidgin English". In PhiN 36, Pp.

Njoke, A. 1996. "Diversity in Cameroon English Pronunciation: A case study of the most-heard users", Unpublished M.A. (Maître) thesis, University of Yaounde 1.

Ntumboh, E. 1998. "The Attitudes towards, and Perception of, Cameroon English Pronunciation". Unpublished postgraduate memoir, ENS Yaounde, University of Yaounde I.

O`Conner, J.D. 1984. *Better English Pronunciation*. Cambridge: Cambridedge University Press.

Pederson, L. 1993. "An Approach to Linguistic Geography". In Preston, D. R. ed. 1993. *American Dialect Research*, Pp. 31-92. Amsterdam: John Benjamins Publishing Co.

Peil, M. 1982. *Social Science Research Methods*. London: Routledge.

Phillips, E. M. and D. S. Pugh. 1987. *How to Get a Ph.D*. Milton Keynes: Open University Press.

Platt, J. 1984. "Englishes in Singapore, Malaysia and Hong kong". In Bailey and Görlach 1984, Pp. 383-414.

___ and M. L. Ho 1984. *The New Englishes*. London: Routlege and Kegan Paul.

Prator, C. 1968. The British Heresy in TESL. In Fishman, J. A., C. A. Ferguson, and D. G. Jyotirindra. eds., Pp. 459-476.

Preston, D. 1985. "Fifty-some old categories of language variation". In *International Journal of the Sociology of Language*, Vol. 57, Pp. 9-47.

Pride, J. B. and J. Holmes. ed. 1972. *Sociolinguistics*. Harmondsword: Penguin Books Ltd.

Rickford, J. R. 1996. "Regional and Social Variation". In Mckay, S. L. and Hornberger. eds. 1996. *Sociolinguistics and Language Teaching*. Cambridge: Cambridge University Press.

Roach, J. 1983. *English Phonetics and Phonology: A practical course*. Cambridge: Cambridge University Press.

Rogers, C. 1955. "Persons or Science: A Philosophical question". In *American Psychologist*, Vol. 10, Pp. 267-279.

Rogers, H. 1991. *Theoretical and Practical Phonetics*. Toronto: Copp Clark Pitman.

Romaine, S. ed. 1982. *Sociolinguistic Variation in Speech Communities*. London: Edward Arnold.

Rudestam, K. E. and R. R. Newton. 1992. *Surviving Your Dissertation: A comprehensive guide to content and process*. London: Sage Publications, Inc.

Sab, N. 1988. "Variation in Cameroon English Pronunciation: A case study of media English". Unpublished Maitrise thesis, University of Yaounde.

Salam, A. M. 1980. "Phonological variation in educated spoken Arabic: a study of the uvular and related plosive types'. In *Bulletin of the school of Oriental and African Studies*. Vol. XLII, Pp.77-100.

Sankoff, D. and G. Sankoff. 1973. "Sample survey methods and computer assisted analysis in the study of grammatical variation". In Darnell, R. ed. 1973. *Canadian Languages in their Social Contexts*, 7-64. Edmonton: Linguistic Research Inc.

___ H. Cedergren; W. Kemp, P. Thibault and D. Vincent. 1989. 'Montreal French: Language, Class and Ideology". In Fasold, R. and D. Schiffrin. 1989. eds. *Language Change and Variation*, Pp. 107-118. Amsterdam: John Benjamins Publishing Company.

Sapir, E. 1929. "The Status of Linguistics as a Science". In *Language*. Vol. 5 Pp. 207-214. In *Selected Writings of Edward Sapir in Language, Culture and Personality*.1968. Mandelbaum, D. G. ed. Berkeley: University of California Press, Pp. 160-166.

Schmidt, Richard W. 1974. "Sociolinguistic Variation in Spoken Arabic in Egypt: A Re-Examination of the Concept of Diglossia". A Ph.D. dissertation, Brown University.

Schmied, J. 1990. "Language Use, Attitudes, Performance and Sociolinguistic Background: A study of English in Kenya, Tanzania, and Zambia". In *English World-Wide*, Vol. 11, No.2, Pp. 217-238.

___ 1991. *English in Africa*. New York: Longman.

Sey, K. A. 1973. *Ghanaian English*. London: Macmillan.

Spencer, J. ed. 1971. *The English language in West Africa*. London: Longman.

Stewtnam, D. 1997. *Writing your Dissertation: How to plan, Prepare and Present your Work Successfully*. UK: Cromwell.

Taiyon, L. C. B. 1985. "Camspeak: A Speech Reality in Cameroon". Unpublished Maitrise thesis, University of Yaounde.

Talbot, E. N. and D. J. Anand. 1950. *General Psychology*. New York: Harper and Row.

Talom, P. 1992. "The Intelligibility of some RP forms in Cameroon". Unpublished Post Graduate Dissertation, ENS, Univ. of Yaounde.

Taylor, D. S. 1996. "Demystifying word stress". In *English Today*, Vol. 12, No. 4, Pp. 46-52.

Taylor, David C., and C. Ounsted. 1972. "The nature of gender differences explored through ontogenetic analyses of sex ratio in disease". In Ounsted, C. and D. C. Taylor 1972. *Gender Differences: Their Ontogeny and Significance*, Pp. 215-240. Edinburgh: Churchill Livingstone.

Tiffen, W. B. 1974. "The Intelligibility of Nigerian English", Unpublished Ph.D. dissertation, University of London.

Todd, L. 1974. *Pidgin and Creoles*. London: Routledge.

___ and I. F. Hancock. 1986. *International English Usage*. London: Croom Helm.

___ 1991. *Talk Pidgin. A structured course in West African Pidgin English*. Leeds: Tortoise Books.

____ 1999. "Global English". In *English Today*, Vol. 15, No. 2, Pp. 30-31.

Tomy, G. ed. 1996. *Research Methods*. London: Arnold.

Tripathi, Prayag D. April 1999. "Growing an International Language". In *English Today*. Vol. 15, N°. 2.

Trudgill, P.1972. "Sex, Covert Prestige and Linguistic Change in the Urban British English of Norwich". In *Language in Society*. Vol. 1, Pp. 179-196.

____ 1974. *Sociolinguistics: An Introduction*. Harmondsworth: Penguin Books Ltd.

____ 1974. *The Social Differentiation of English in Norwich*. Cambridge: Cambridge University Press.

____ ed. 1978. *Sociolinguistic Patterns in British English*. London: Edward Arnold.

____ 1983. *Sociolinguistics: An Introduction to Language and Society*. London: Penguin Group Publishers.

____ and J. Hannah. 1985. *International English: A Guide to Varieties of Standard English*. London: Edward Arnold University Press.

Wolfram, W. 1969. *A Sociolinguistic Description of Detroit Negro Speech*. Washington, DC: Center for Applied Linguistics.

____ 1993. "Identifying and Interpreting Variables". In Preston, R. D. ed. 1993. *American Dialect Research*. Pp.193-221. Amsterdam: John Benjamin's Publishing Co.

Yule, G. 1985. *The Study of Language*. Cambridge: Cambridge University Press.

B E R K E L E Y
I N S I G H T S
IN LINGUISTICS
AND SEMIOTICS

Irmengard Rauch
General Editor

Through the publication of groundbreaking scholarly research, this series deals with language and the multiple and varied paradigms through which it is studied. Language as viewed by linguists represents micrometa-approaches that intersect with macrometa-approaches of semiotists who understand language as an inlay to all experience. This data-based series bridges study of the sciences with that of the humanities.

To order other books in this series, please contact our Customer Service Department at:

800-770-LANG (within the U.S.)
212-647-7706 (outside the U.S.)
212-647-7707 FAX
CustomerService@plang.com

Or browse online by series at:
www.peterlang.com